# Globalization and Industrial Development

# Globalization and Industrial Development

*Junmo Kim*
*KonKuk University, Seoul, Korea*

iUniverse, Inc.
New York Lincoln Shanghai

# Globalization and Industrial Development

iUniverse books may be ordered through booksellers or by contacting:

iUniverse
2021 Pine Lake Road, Suite 100
Lincoln, NE 68512
www.iuniverse.com
1-800-Authors (1-800-288-4677)


ISBN-13: 978-0-595-36098-7 (pbk)
ISBN-13: 978-0-595-80544-0 (ebk)
ISBN-10: 0-595-36098-X (pbk)
ISBN-10: 0-595-80544-2 (ebk)

Printed in the United States of America

To my Lord, Jesus Christ

# Contents

List of Illustrations . . . . . . . . . . . . . . . . . . . . . . . . . . . . . . . . . . . . . . ix

List of Tables . . . . . . . . . . . . . . . . . . . . . . . . . . . . . . . . . . . . . . . . xiii

Preface . . . . . . . . . . . . . . . . . . . . . . . . . . . . . . . . . . . . . . . . . . . . . xv

CHAPTER 1    Introduction . . . . . . . . . . . . . . . . . . . . . . . . . . . . . . .1

CHAPTER 2    International Comparison of Industry Performance . . .15

CHAPTER 3    Dynamics of Regional Research Clusters . . . . . . . . . . .59

CHAPTER 4    Dynamics of Innovation Network Building between
Research Institutions and Small & Medium
Enterprises(SME)s . . . . . . . . . . . . . . . . . . . . . . . . . . .80

CHAPTER 5    Targeting the Future . . . . . . . . . . . . . . . . . . . . . . . . .98

CHAPTER 6    Globalization of the Public Sector: A Social Capital
Perspective . . . . . . . . . . . . . . . . . . . . . . . . . . . . . . . .115

CHAPTER 7    Conclusion . . . . . . . . . . . . . . . . . . . . . . . . . . . . . .136

APPENDIX     Cluster Analysis and Discriminant Analysis on industrial
wage data: Procedures in Mathematical Illustration . . . .139

Bibliography . . . . . . . . . . . . . . . . . . . . . . . . . . . . . . . . . . . . . . .143

Index . . . . . . . . . . . . . . . . . . . . . . . . . . . . . . . . . . . . . . . . . . . .161

# List of Illustrations

*Figure 2-1 Cluster Result of Economic Integration (1985-1994)* . . . . . . . . . . . . . . . . .*21*

*Figure 2-2 A Two Group Structure within the European Group* . . . . . . . . . . . . . . . . . .*22*

*Figure 2-3 The Pan-Pacific Group.* . . . . . . . . . . . . . . . . . . . . . . . . . . . . . . . . . . . . . . . .*22*

*Figure 2-4 Cluster Result of Economic Integration (1985-2001)* . . . . . . . . . . . . . . . . .*23*

*Figure 2-5 Cluster Result for Textile Industry (1985-1994)* . . . . . . . . . . . . . . . . . . . . .*24*

*Figure 2-6 Cluster Result for Textile Industry (1985-2001)* . . . . . . . . . . . . . . . . . . . . .*25*

*Figure 2-7 Times Series Plotting of U.S. Money and the First Root (Textile)* . . . . . . . .*55*

*Figure 2-8 Industry Performance (Textile Industry) (1985-1994)* . . . . . . . . . . . . . . . .*26*

*Figure 2-9 Industry Performance by economic groups (Textile Industry)
(1990-2000)* . . . . . . . . . . . . . . . . . . . . . . . . . . . . . . . . . . . . . . . . . . . . . . . .*27*

*Figure 2-10 Cluster Result for Auto Industry (1985-1994)* . . . . . . . . . . . . . . . . . . . . .*28*

*Figure 2-11 Cluster Result for Auto Industry (1985-2001)* . . . . . . . . . . . . . . . . . . . . .*28*

*Figure 2-12 Times Series Plotting of U.S. Money and the First Root (Auto)* . . . . . . . .*56*

*Figure 2-13 Industry Performance by Economic Groups (Auto Industry)
(1985-1994)* . . . . . . . . . . . . . . . . . . . . . . . . . . . . . . . . . . . . . . . . . . . . . . . .*30*

*Figure 2-14 Industry Performance by Economic Groups (Auto Industry)
(1992-2000)* . . . . . . . . . . . . . . . . . . . . . . . . . . . . . . . . . . . . . . . . . . . . . . . .*30*

*Figure 2-15 Cluster Result for Fabricated Metal & Machinery Industry
(1985-1994)* . . . . . . . . . . . . . . . . . . . . . . . . . . . . . . . . . . . . . . . . . . . . . . . .*32*

*Figure 2-16 Cluster Result for Fabricated Metal & Machinery Industry
(1985-2001)* . . . . . . . . . . . . . . . . . . . . . . . . . . . . . . . . . . . . . . . . . . . . . . . .*33*

*Figure 2-17 Times Series Plotting of U.S. Money and the First Root (Fab. Metal &*
*Machinery)* . . . . . . . . . . . . . . . . . . . . . . . . . . . . . . . . . . . . . . . . . . . . . . . . . . *56*

*Figure 2-18 Industry Performance by Economic Groups (Fabricated Metal &*
*Machinery) (1985-1994)* . . . . . . . . . . . . . . . . . . . . . . . . . . . . . . . . . . . . . . *34*

*Figure 2-19 Industry Performance by Economic Groups (Fabricated Metal &*
*Machinery) (1991-2000)* . . . . . . . . . . . . . . . . . . . . . . . . . . . . . . . . . . . . . . *35*

*Figure 2-20 Cluster Result for Industrial & Commercial Machinery Industry*
*(1985-1994)* . . . . . . . . . . . . . . . . . . . . . . . . . . . . . . . . . . . . . . . . . . . . . . . . *36*

*Figure 2-21 Cluster Result for Industrial Machinery Industry (1985-2001)* . . . . . . . *37*

*Figure 2-22 Times Series Plotting of U.S. Money and the First Root (Industrial &*
*Commercial Machinery)* . . . . . . . . . . . . . . . . . . . . . . . . . . . . . . . . . . . . . . . *57*

*Figure 2-23 Industry Performance by Economic Groups (Industrial & Commercial*
*Machinery industry) (1985-1994)* . . . . . . . . . . . . . . . . . . . . . . . . . . . . . . . *38*

*Figure 2-24 Industry Performance by Economic Groups (Industrial & Commercial*
*Machinery industry) (1989-2001)* . . . . . . . . . . . . . . . . . . . . . . . . . . . . . . . *39*

*Figure 2-25 Cluster Result for Shipbuilding & Repair Industry (1985-1994)* . . . . . . *40*

*Figure 2-26 Cluster Result for Shipbuilding & Repair Industry (1985-2001)* . . . . . . *41*

*Figure 2-27 Times Series Plotting of U.S. Money and the First Root (Ship)* . . . . . . . . *57*

*Figure 2-28 Industry Performance by Economic Groups (Shipbuilding &Repair*
*Industry) (1985-1994)* . . . . . . . . . . . . . . . . . . . . . . . . . . . . . . . . . . . . . . . . *42*

*Figure 2-29 Industry Performance by Economic Groups(Shipbuilding & Repair*
*Industry) (1992-2000)* . . . . . . . . . . . . . . . . . . . . . . . . . . . . . . . . . . . . . . . . *43*

*Figure 2-30 International Market Share of major Shipbuilding Nations (New Ship*
*building orders in Tonnage)* . . . . . . . . . . . . . . . . . . . . . . . . . . . . . . . . . . . . *44*

*Figure 2-31 Cluster Result for Electronics Industry (1985-1994)* . . . . . . . . . . . . . . . . *45*

*Figure 2-32 Cluster Result for Electronics Industry (1985-2001)* . . . . . . . . . . . . . . . . *46*

*Figure 2-33 Times Series Plotting of U.S. Money and the First Root (Electronics)* . . . *58*

*Figure 2-34 Industry Performance by Economic Groups (Electronics Industry)*
*(1985-1994)* . . . . . . . . . . . . . . . . . . . . . . . . . . . . . . . . . . . . . . . . . . . . . . . . *47*

*Figure 2-35 Industry Performance by Economic Groups (Electronics Industry) The*
*Second Root Plotting (1990-2001)* . . . . . . . . . . . . . . . . . . . . . . . . . . . . . . . *48*

*Figure 2-36 Cluster Result for Primary Metal Industry (1985-2001)* . . . . . . . . . . . . . *49*

*Figure 2-37 Times Series Plotting of U.S. Money and the First Root (Primary Metal)*. . . . . . . . . . . . . . . . . . . . . . . . . . . . . . . . . . . . . . . . . . . . . . . . . . . *58*

*Figure 2-38 Industry Performance by Economic Groups (Primary Metal) (1990-2001)* . . . . . . . . . . . . . . . . . . . . . . . . . . . . . . . . . . . . . . . . . . . . *50*

*Figure 3-1 Adjacent Municipalities around the Sophia Antipolis*. . . . . . . . . . . . . . . . . *77*

*Figure 5-1 Cluster diagram of the digital Infra structure in Korea 1989-2000 (supply side)* . . . . . . . . . . . . . . . . . . . . . . . . . . . . . . . . . . . . . . . . . . *107*

*Figure 5-2 Household expenditure growth pattern (1993-1999)*. . . . . . . . . . . . . . . . . *108*

*Figure 5-3 Annual Investment and the First Root Matching* . . . . . . . . . . . . . . . . . . . *109*

*Figure 5-4 Annual Investment Root and the Cumulative Increase of Production Index(Vertical)* . . . . . . . . . . . . . . . . . . . . . . . . . . . . . . . . . . . . . . . . . . . . *110*

*Figure 6-1 Globalization and Government Performance*. . . . . . . . . . . . . . . . . . . . . . . *125*

*Figure 6-2 A Simple Organizational chart to explain reform*. . . . . . . . . . . . . . . . . . . . *134*

# List of Tables

*Table 1-1 Annual Average growth of Industrial Production for Selected Countries* . . . . . 7

*Table 1-2 Annual Average Growth rate for service sector for Selected Countries* . . . . . . . 8

*Table 2-1 World Automobile production (in million units)* . . . . . . . . . . . . . . . . . . . . . 31

*Table 2-2 Export Performance of General Machinery* . . . . . . . . . . . . . . . . . . . . . . . . . 35

*Table 2–3 Summary of Findings from 1985-1994 analysis* . . . . . . . . . . . . . . . . . . . . . . 52

*Table 2-4  Summary of Findings from 1990-2001 analysis.* . . . . . . . . . . . . . . . . . . . . . 53

*Table 2-5 Major Auto Manufacturing Groups.* . . . . . . . . . . . . . . . . . . . . . . . . . . . . . 54

*Table 3-1 Total employment by types of firms in Kista District 1990-2004* . . . . . . . . 74

*Table 4–1 R&D Model I: Generational Typology I.* . . . . . . . . . . . . . . . . . . . . . . . . . . 83

*Tabel 4-2 R&D Model II: Generational Typology II* . . . . . . . . . . . . . . . . . . . . . . . . . 84

*Table 4-3 Logit Results from Model 1-1(Research Institutions with Direct
question)* . . . . . . . . . . . . . . . . . . . . . . . . . . . . . . . . . . . . . . . . . . . . . . . . 94

*Table 4-4 Logit Results from Model 1-2(Research Institutions with Indirect
question)* . . . . . . . . . . . . . . . . . . . . . . . . . . . . . . . . . . . . . . . . . . . . . . . . 94

*Table 4-5 Logit Results from Model 2 (SMEs)* . . . . . . . . . . . . . . . . . . . . . . . . . . . . . 95

*Table 5-1 Universal Tools of Industrial Policy.* . . . . . . . . . . . . . . . . . . . . . . . . . . . . 100

*Table 5-2 Profile of Communications Equipment Industry* . . . . . . . . . . . . . . . . . . . . 102

*Table 5-3 Proportion of PC production and marketdistribution.* . . . . . . . . . . . . . . . . 104

*Table 5-4 Market Structure of Korea's PC market* . . . . . . . . . . . . . . . . . . . . . . . . . . 104

*Table 6-1 Conducive vs. Negative factors for Social Capital* . . . . . . . . . . . . . . . . . . . 119

# *Preface*

Globalization has been, in some sense, one of the most widely discussed concept in understanding social, economic, and political aspects of the changing world since the late 20<sup>th</sup> century on. This book, noting the phenomenon, focuses on two parts. One is to empirically track industry level performance of major selected industrial sectors with an aim to analyze the existence of economic bloc formation. The other is more policy oriented one, which is to present exemplars or areas where public & private actors together work on for economic & industrial development.

Existing literature has discussed on how economic integration was brought about from economic and political contexts. What is lacking in these traditions is more empirically founded research that would provide support for their arguments. This book, noting the necessity, tackles this point. Especially, this book questions whether there has been a common economic dynamic that has driven the economic integration. If there is any common economic dynamic per se that has had major impact on globalization and integration, this paper can present how different industrial sectors of different regions are affected, and thereby provide clues to fill the gaps in the existing theories.

While part I of this book is to approach an empirical data analysis at both macro and micro level industry analysis, part II of the book seeks policy oriented endeavors. Against the backdrop of globalization, there has been a developing trend of convergence of policy instruments and contents across countries due to a commonly shared notion of the importance of R&D. The notion that R&D has been the source of economic growth has evoked a policy idea to promote national and regional level R&D networks. In pursuing the ideas, actual mechanisms & tools of R&D networks, it is possible to admit difficulties and limitations in designing and implementing policies. Before going into the discussion on National and Regional R&D system, it is pivotal to address on why different regions and countries began focusing on research networks for their solution for R&D and economic growth. These policies range from incentive based policies, including monetary and non-monetary policies to regulation policies either monetary regulation related or market entry regulation type. In fact, designing and implementing new policies, namely national R&D policies, would also utilize some combination, or, in the extreme case, all the policy measures. This sensitive nature increases delicacy and reduces potentials for success. This has been the reason to focus on policy issues in part II by presenting an array of different policy issues that fall into the areas of R&D policies.

This book has another dimension in personal academic pursuit as well. This year marks the 8th year since my graduation of Ph.D. program, and this book is the second sole authored book since my graduation. After graduation, I had experiences at two government funded research institutions before joining my current academic position, which directly and indirectly has influenced the contents in this book. The publication of this book allows an invaluable milestone in the sense that it gives an opportunity to reflect the recent years of research and suggests a new momentum for future research directions. Upon publishing this book, I would like to express deep gratitude to my teachers. I would like to express my gratitude to Professor James K. Galbraith of LBJ School of Public Affairs at the University of Texas at Austin and Professor Victoria Rodriguez, who is now Vice Provost at the University of Texas at Austin. My deep gratitude extends to Professor Manuel Heitor of Instituto Superior Technico in Portugal, Professor M. Dorgham of International Centre for Technology and Management, Professor Robert H. Wilson, and Professor Chandler Stolp at LBJ School for their professional advice during my odyssey of research. Above all, I would like to express my deepest gratitude to my Lord Jesus Christ for allowing my meetings with the above mentioned people. Though not mentioned, I believe that there are many other significant persons who have given positive encouragements to my life and research. Finally, I would like to express deep gratitude to my wife Hyeree and my four kids, Gyu-Young, Ah-Young, Je-Hyun, and Je-Yoon, who have extended externalities of joy while writing this book.

# 1

# Introduction

## Prologue

Globalization has been, in some sense, one of the most widely discussed concept in understanding social, economic, and political aspects of the changing world since the late 20th century. This book, noting the phenomenon, focuses on two parts. One is to empirically track industry level performance of major selected industrial sectors with an aim to analyze the existence of economic bloc formation. The second focal point is more policy oriented one, which is to present exemplars or areas where public & private actors together work on for economic & industrial development.

Regarding the first point, as a discourse ranging from academic circle to business community and government & international circles, globalization has been mainly discussed in the existing literature in the three following streams. The first stream has been a macro economic approach with country level data. The second approach has been a discourse in political aspects of economic integration. The third one, in comparison, has been micro economic approach to deal with trade structure between countries and regions, especially focusing on the impact of forming a free trade agreement or related regimes. Among these, it is possible to summarize the economic and political side arguments in the below.

### *Economic Determinism: Interdependence and Transaction Costs*

While a Marxist tradition argues that economic integration as a resolution to cope with contradictions of capitalist world (Cocks 1980), theorists in economic determinism or globalization show their intellectual tradition much closer to the neoclassical economic theory. It is this vein that the economic integration school finds that expansion of markets due from developments in science & technology and its application in communication & transportation as the major cause that brought economic integration (Keohane & Nye 1977; Geoffrey 1998). In other words, changes in socio-economic backgrounds increased market size and interdependence among countries, which resulted in the formation of major economic blocs.

To the scholars, increased interdependence could be interpreted in terms of transaction costs (McKay 1996). When transaction costs are negligible, compared to gains from international transactions, it is natural to expand trade. If, however, transaction costs are substantial or distributed unequally among trading countries, it would be relatively small countries that would favor institutional framework to reduce vulnerability. Economic integration is considered as one of the institutional arrangement in this context. To elaborate the idea, the following can be suggested. Since the 1950s, according to economic determinism, the World economy has experienced structural changes. Especially, in Europe, individual countries have built a consensus that it would be in their interests to integrate in managing inflation and stability of currency (Brummer 1993; Levi 1987).

As a critique, economic determinism has its weakness in that it regards inter-relationship between economy and politics as a causal relationship. To establish a causal relationship, it is important to provide how the causal link can be established. Also, it is essential to show micro-economic or industry level evidence to support the dynamic of integration. Economic determinism lacks sufficient conditions to be a causal explanation. and leaves much room for empirical works.

### Political Determinism

Political determinism, in contrast to economic determinism, emphasizes capacity and will of politics in forming economic integration. Among diverse views in this category, theorists in inter-governmentalism claims that participation into economic integration is determined by national interests and that national interests are defined by the position of a country in the international system (Waltz 1979). In comparison, another branch argues that national interests are defined by domestic politics (Bulmer 1983). These political explanations were not sufficient enough to persuade readers on how economic integration was accomplished. Inter-governmentalism assumes that government represents national interests on a monopolistic basis excluding societal influence. Therefore, if there is any possibility that Non-governmental organizations (NGOs) or interests in international arena can be established, monopolistic position of the government would be reduced. In contrast, theorists of domestic politics are not free from critiques, since domestic politics was regarded as a reflection of domestic industrial and economic interests and thereby repeating the logic of economic determinism.

As shown above, existing literature has discussed on how economic integration was brought about from economic and political contexts. What is lacking in these traditions is more empirically founded research that would provide support for their arguments. Furthermore, an empirically based research in itself finds room for its own appeal when it can present a spectrum of different industrial and interests gaining and losing with the advent of economic integration. This paper, noting the necessity, tackles this point. Especially, this paper questions whether there has been a common economic dynamic that has driven the economic integration. Also, this research presents a wider scope than the existing literature in the sense that countries included range from European to Asian countries. If there is any common economic dynamic per se that has had major impact on globalization and integration, this paper can present how different industrial sectors of different regions are affected, and thereby provide clues to fill the gaps in the existing theories.

## Traditional Role of Government in promoting Economy & Industry

After analyzing industry & country level economic performance in wage analysis in Part I, this book, as mentioned is geared toward presenting the new roles & areas of government and private actors in promoting economy & industry. Thus, before discussing the new roles & areas, it is essential to show the traditional roles & tools of government in the promotion of economy & industry.

As presented in table 5-1, in chapter 5, policy measures for industrial promotion can be divided into two groups, incentives and regulation, which can be applied to virtually every industrial sector for all governments. Among incentive policies, it is possible to distinguish between policies of monetary incentives and those with non-monetary incentives. Policies of monetary incentives are, in fact, known to take the lion's share when one discusses the contents of industrial policy in many countries. Inside the umbrella of industrial policy of monetary incentives, there is a quite wide spectrum of policies, ranging from tax credits, finance to demand creation and infra structure building including social infra structure.(Lee 1996) Among them, tax incentives and finance measures are regarded as controversial in the sense that these policies may distort the economy with the "visible hands of government".(Kim, J. 2002; Norton, R.D.1986) Separate from the theoretical debate on its harmful effects, this type of policies have been in practice in many developing countries including Korea (Kim, J. 2002;Galbraith & Kim 2001). It is also a common finding that as an economy develops in its size and mode of governance from government-led to private sector-led, direct measures of industrial policy are reduced in relative terms (Sakong 1987; Galbraith & Kim 1998). Regarding IT sector promotion, if a country's policy is linked to annual investment of the country, it would be fair to understand that the country's policies include incentive policies of monetary nature.

In comparison, policies of demand creation and social infra structure building are clearly less market distorting than the other type of incentive policy. One thing to note, however, is that in utilizing demand creation policy, financial capacity and mechanism of a country determines the extent of the policy in that country. For example, limits of credit lines allowable to firms and households are examples that demand policy can be operated within. In promoting IT sector in Korea, the Korean government has wisely utilized the demand creation policy. An earlier example of this policy is found in the case of personal computer industry promotion in the early 1980s, at which time the Korean industry was in its infant stage. The way the policy worked was that the demand creation was made by making educational needs of students. At this time, a policy example was to host computer skills contest for elementary schools students whose parents were forced to expend on PCs. After the initial promotion, IBM compatible PCs were in great demand for teenagers through the 1990s.

Non-monetary incentive policies include "vision statement policy" (Norton 1986), building cooperative networks (Kim, J. 1999), and promotion of competition. The vision statement policy is valid in the sense that private sector receives the direction of the government in the way the government will manage the economy in the future. Building cooperative networks have been widely in use, as exemplified in SEMATECH and numerous consortium schemes in Japan (Kim, J. 1999; Anchordoguy, M 1988). In regulation policies, market entrance regulation has been a very strong policy tool of government including the Korean case. As was the case in other sectoral promotion, regulating the number of firms has been in practice in cellular phone service market, which can be an example of the policy. (Kim, J. 2002)

## Contexts for Change

Against the existing roles & tools, it is possible to present contexts for changes in approaching the growth of economy & industry, which does not mean that the traditional roles & areas of government are nullified. The hints for the changing contexts can be suggested by the tables in the below.

### *General Economic conditions*

In advanced industrialized countries, it has been widely understood that momentum for growth has been in down turn modes. Starting from manufacturing sectors, the trend has spread to other sectors as service sector. As shown in table 1-1, the Average Annual growth rates of Industrial Production for Selected Countries have shown a mild convergence within the range of 3 to 4 percent since 1980s on. The trend has also been found in service sector, as seen in table 1-2. Against the plateau like economic phenomenon, different theories have offered only partial explanations.

### *Productivity Paradox argument*

There has been a challenging argument to explain the stagnated economic growth phenomenon, the productivity paradox (Kim, J. 2005; Perez & Freeman 1988; Krugman 1996). Historically since the post world war II era, capitalism has passed through the "matured" mass production system regime (Boltho 1982), and then continued its track of development. Symptoms of this change can be articulated as follows. First, one could observe the advent of knowledge economy (Drucker, P. 2002), which requires heavier contents of knowledge from research to production. Second, it was possible to find the increase of service sectors including the high value adding service sectors (Hansen, N.2002). Underlying these symptoms is a common dynamic that advanced economies began requiring longer and more complex linkages from knowledge(or research) to the actual production of goods and services (Bell, G. 1990). As mentioned, as the nature of capitalism has required more intensified knowledge & capital requirements, the answer from the economy was to increase R&D to "ride" the dynamic of "intensified" capital requirements.

The problem arose, since the causal linkage, from R&D efforts to the actual outcome that is economically meaningful, is becoming harder and harder to track; in conventional numeric, a thoughtful economist should have to "confess" that productivity at the industry or societal level seems to be decreased as the R&D budget increases(McCune, J. 1998; McSheehy, J. 2001; Perez, C. and C. Freeman 1988) This is the dynamic of productivity paradox (Kim, J. 2005) so far experienced in the advanced economies (Banks, E. 1998; Pinsonneault, A & Rivard 1998; Anderson, P.1997). Turning our attention to the Korean case, the phenomenon can be broadly applied, since the economy has undergone a change to a more knowledge and R&D intensive structure compared to the past.

## Business Confidence Argument

In explaining the post World War Two growth in the Western European settings, in Boltho's view, it is government's adoption of Keynesianism that maintained business confidence. Similarly, in Schonfield's observation, planning (Driscoll 1984) had an "assuring" function in the French economy during the 1950s and 1960s (Shonfield 1965). The importance of the Keynesian demand management policies introduced in the post World War II era was that business could have confidence in government's ability to control economic downswings. These theorists, based on their notion of strong business confidence, propose a causal link between the dramatic increase in investment after World War II and the super growth of Western Europe in that period. The average investment ratio for Europe between 1950 and 1970 was 16.8%, compared to 9.6% in the 1928-1938 period of inter war years in Europe (Boltho 1982). For these authors, the essence of the business investment decision was the expectations of future profits. The increase in investment over the interwar year level, thus, was interpreted as a reflection of the increase in the entrepreneurs' degree of confidence. Government was believed to be capable of softening and even controlling the boom and bust of business cycles with the use of counter-cyclical policy instruments. Similarly, in the French case, indicative planning has been the backbone that maintained and bolstered business confidence.

While admitting the efficacy of the approach, it is not still clear what determines business confidence. A more serious drawback to this explanation is its treatment of the economic crisis in Europe in the 1970s. Since the explanation of the economic development was built around the notion of business confidence, the economic crisis was also explained by the disintegration of the confidence. Despite the weaknesses of this theory, however, it provides an embryonic element in theorizing business-government relations (Shonfield 1965).

## Neo-Marxist argument

O'Connor argued that the growth of the State is both a cause and an effect of the expansion of the monopoly capital, or big business that enjoys monopolistic status. In his framework, the State and its bureaucracy are willing to hear and provide what business demands (Block, F 1977, 1980). In O'Connor's analysis of the capitalist world, three types of industries exist. The competitive sector is where small firms are located; the monopoly sector is the area of large firms; the State sector is organized either by the State itself or organized by industries under contract with the State. In this theory, the monopoly sector is undeniably the engine for the growth. It needs to externalize its production costs, and thus it has clear policy preferences: government should expand social expense outlays such as defense contracts (O'Connor 1970; Magdoff 1969); also, the monopoly sector favors socializing social consumption expenditures, such as medical costs and workers' retirement funds (O'Connor 1973). Furthermore, the monopoly sector wants the growth of State-financed social investment, which is for infra-structure. In their policy preferences, the functional Marxist view sees an alliance between the capital and labor. The State cannot but listen to the monopoly sector, since it bears the main thrust of economic growth. This is the point where, in the functional Marxist view, Schumpeterian optimism for capitalism is denied (O'Connor 1973) and replaced by a permanent crisis (Pryke 1966). Against the demand for externalization of costs by the monopoly sector, the relationship between the State and the monopoly sector is formed in a symbiotic manner.

**Table 1-1 Annual Average growth of Industrial Production for Selected Countries** [*]

| | | | |
|---|---|---|---|
| Portugal | 1992~1996 | 1996~1997 | 1997~2001 |
| | 2.09 | | |
| France | 1995~1997 | 1998~2000 | 2000~2001 |
| | 2.09 | 3.50 | 3.20 |
| Italy | 1994~1997 | 1997~1998 | 1998~2001 |
| | 2.60 | 1.86 | 1.87 |

**Table 1-1 Annual Average growth of Industrial Production for Selected Countries (Continued)***

| Spain | 1991~1994 | 1994~1995 | | 1995~1999 |
|---|---|---|---|---|
| | -0.11 | 4.71 | | 3.07 |
| Japan | 1983~1988 | 1988~1994 | 1994-1999 | 1999-2001 |
| | 5.23 | 0.28 | 0.78 | 6.3 |

* note :Average of the period, *1995 price
Source : IMF, International Financial Statistics Yearbook, 2001.

In the tradition of the Regulation school and related theorists, scholars like Boyer, Michael Piore & Charles Sabel (Piore & Sabel 1984; Sabel 1984) diagnosed the crisis of capitalism as the outgrown symptom of the world capitalist system. In this line of intellectual reasoning, a natural consequence and a remedy are regional policies and politics, especially coupled with Sabel's flexible specialization theory.

**Table 1-2 Annual Average Growth rate for service sector for Selected Countries ***

| Portugal | 1992~1996 | 1996~1997 | | 1997~2001 |
|---|---|---|---|---|
| | - | 2.8 | | 4.84 |
| France | 1995~1997 | 1998~2000 | | 2000~2001 |
| | 1.70 | 3.30 | | 2.11 |
| Italy | 1994~1997 | 1997~1998 | | 1998~2001 |
| | 1.95 | 1.96 | | 2.49 |
| Spain | 1991~1994 | 1994~1995 | | 1995~1999 |
| | 0.79 | 2.58 | | 2.93 |
| Japan | 1983~1988 | 1988~1994 | 1994-1999 | 1999-2001 |
| | 3.92 | 4.48 | 3.47 | |

* Note:average of the period, *1995 price
Source: OECD, Quarterly National Accounts2001.

## Rational Choice Argument

In the intellectual tradition of so-called the "rational choice" and rational choice institutionalism, including the harbingers of the theory like Olson's, there is another unique line of explanation on the sluggish economic performance (Olson, M. 1982). Olson builds his own political economy based explanation from his earlier writing (Olson, M. 1962) to later one by connecting them by crossing the unit of analysis in the two different work pieces in an elegant way. Olson starts from his argument on group politics.

Mancur Olson offers an attack on the pluralist notion of the role of interest groups and politics, and suggests how, and under what situations collective goods (political interests) can be provided, Olson offers a notion that is against the pluralist model that any interest can be mobilized and organized in a society. In Olsonian world, only small groups and large groups that can supply selective incentives can be mobilized and maintained as interest organizations. In the pluralistic picture, it has been assumed that citizens with a common political interest would organize and lobby to serve their interests. David Truman's concept of "potential interests" shows this possibility. Furthermore, because each individual is engaged in more than one group, which is called as cross-cutting situation and the consequence of the cross-cutting is a vectoring of pressures of group competition, societal stability is attained in the pluralism. The vectoring of pressures explained the outcomes of the political process in American politics.

From this context, it was natural to extend that if workers, farmers, or consumers faced monopolies harmful to their interests, they would eventually attain countervailing power through organizations such as labor unions or farm organizations that obtained market power and protective government action. In Olsonian view, the pluralistic view does not happen, due to the "collective action problem"; this problem stems from "rational individuals" In a hypothetical case, the very fact that the objective or interest is common to or shared by the group entails that the gain from any sacrifice an individual makes to serve this common purpose is shared with everyone in the group. So the individual in any large group with a common interest will reap only a minute share of the gains from what ever sacrifices the individual makes to achieve this common interest. From the notion of rational individuals, Olson draws "free-rider" problem; no one will sacrifice, and they hoped to be a free rider. A consequence is no mobilization.

Olson argues that any large interest groups need selective incentives other than collective goods for their existence and maintenance. Union dues are an example of negative selective incentives, while American farm organizations usually offer positive selective incentives. From the above reasoning, Olson suggests the following generalization: Other things being equal, the larger the number of individuals or firms that would benefit from a collective good, the smaller the share of the gains from action in the group interest that will accrue to the individual or firm that undertakes the action. Thus, in the absence of selective incentives, the incentive for group action diminishes as group size increases, so that large groups are less able to act in their interests than the small ones.

Quite intriguing was how Olson links his argument on macro economic performance of the major industrialized countries with his notion of group politics. In his book of 1982, he argued that countries in which interest groups have been "destroyed" either by war or other forces, due to the nature of group politics and reduced costs from groups, economic growth has been significantly higher than the countries with strong interest group traditions.

When his argument was first published, it was a shock to intellectual as well as business and other circles due to implications and repercussions that could have arisen from it. Nearly three decades after the argument, it is now clear that his argument was too simplistic in holding water. In succeeding the intellectual tradition, scholars like Douglas North (1990) provides how incentives and disincentives built in institutional arrangements in a society can affect long term economic performance with different historical cases. The notion that has been presented by North and similar scholars clear opens the horizon where academic circles as well as policy makers should put their eyes on in developing regional industrial & economic development. Understanding the link between pure economic realm and the social, economic institutional fabric would suggest ways to improve economic performance, and may offer clues to understand why some regions or countries can maintain sustainable development tracks and the social consensus at the same time under exactly identical economic situation in which other countries and regions suffer in common.

## New Roles & Areas for Public & Private actors

### *Creating Porter's competitive advantage*

Creating competitiveness has become a new role for both private and public bodies all around the world. The concept of cluster has been studied in economic geography in the past, which has not received attention by different groups until Michael Porter style rediscovery gave light to the concept. For Porter, the concept of cluster was a very natural extension of his theory on competitiveness, since cluster concept was imposed on his theory on competitiveness (Porter, M. 1998b). Developed originally from the discipline of geography, cluster theory has received glamorous footlights with the introduction by Michael Porter, who has applied the cluster concept to his notion of Diamond type competitiveness theory (Lagendijk 1997; Yamawaki 2002). Reflecting the origin of cluster that comes from the lineage of theory development(Lorenz & Lawson 1999; Saxenian 1994; Rantisi 2002) from the new industrial district, to networks and RIS, Porter defined a cluster as a network of suppliers, final consumers, user firms, and producers that are linked to production chains, yet maintain independence. Succeeding the popularity and attention on clusters, public discussion on clusters found an exit by converting the concept of clusters into innovation clusters by including the actors of innovation, which are universities, public research institutions, consulting firms, and other knowledge intensive business firms. (OECD 1999b) This can be understood as a definite synthesis of theories aimed at practical application.

While it is also noteworthy that Porter's theory is not without drawbacks, as will be discussed in chapter three of this book, it is also undeniably true that his theory has inspired many concerned audience regarding what to do to create future competitiveness of a region and a country.

### *Science Parks and the RIS/NIS in Knowledge Economy*

Ranging from research complex, Science Park, and Research Park to technopolis, incubation center and technopark, these different names had different starting points, but eventually have grown to mean the identical phenomenon. The reason this type of concept could receive footlights was due to the changed understanding to approach the way science & technology can contribute to the development of economy and industry. Starting from 1960s, the success of the Silicon Valley has inspired enthusiasts of the technopolis to emulate the success case. In so doing, Sophia Antipolis has been a clear example to follow the trend.

In the cases of Sophia Antipolis of France and Tsukuba of Japan, the emphasis has been given primarily to research, in comparison to the Silicon Valley. While Sophia Antipolis has been famous for its vast size, the British adaptation has been a much smaller variant called 'Science Park'(DTI 2001). Through the 1980s, a notable development has been the emphasis given to industrial application of research and knowledge, which naturally turned the development of industrial location to include production side into the existing research oriented sites. In Germany, this trend was exemplified as innovation centers that have been focusing on commercialization of new technologies rather than research (Cooke 1992). Despite this long change pattern, the 1990s gave a unified direction which was to add incubation and housing functions to the research complexes. As described, seemingly different concepts, in fact, have become, de facto, identical phenomenon through the adding of new functions (Kim, L.1997; Swan 1998; OECD 1999a; OECD 2001).

Regional Innovation System has been an adaptation from the notion of national innovation system (Lundvall 2000; Cooke et al. 1997; Cooke 1998c) in the regional settings. As the term system denotes the Regional Innovation System is a system in which all innovation actors, in a regional setting, are integrated in socio-cultural environments. The concept goes beyond a simple boundary of a technopolis or a research park in that it encompasses all arrays of institutions and even education system into the concept. Based on academic consensus, the followings can be understood as the key components of the Regional Innovation System (Maskell & Malecki 2002).

(1) Different types of regional & local networks (Fisher, M. & Snickars 2001)

(2) Group learning & its embedded local & regional culture (Capello 1999; Fritsch, M. 2001)

(3) Trust among economic & social actors that would facilitate the infiltration of innovation into societal roots (Cooke & Morgan 1998; Hudson 1994)

(4) Institutional integrity that is fundamental to entrepreneurship (Fritsch, M. 2001)

(5) External relations that would enable the region to get over the 'lock-in' effect of path-dependency, and thereby opens new avenue & sources for innovation from outside the region

As would be understood by the key components, the trend of theory development has been made into two directions. One was a theoretical tradition that emphasizes the system concept (Lundvall 2000) and the other side can be characterized as that focuses on network itself. (Fisher, M. 1999; Gibson, David 2004; Kim, J. 2002; Keeble et al. 1999)

The grand scheme of the theory of Regional Innovation System allows the theory to have a greater explanatory power. This advantage, however, has a crucial disadvantage found in other theories with 'all powerful' explanatory power, like historical institutionalism found in social science tradition. By encompassing every element that has to do with explanation, the theory of Regional Innovation System has resulted in explaining nothing. In comparison, another branch of Regional Innovation System theory variant, network theories have focused on micro dynamic of networks in innovation systems.

## *Social Capital and the public sector performance*

As economies get more complex in their ways of interacting with internal and external actors, it has become a commonly shared idea that competitiveness of a region or a country, or even an economic bloc would not be de-linked with social environments of the economic entity. Well versed in the cases like the third Italy and the New Industrial District, the main argument of the new industrial district is centered on socio-cultural aspects of location & its formation. Since the root of the new industrial district comes from the Marshallian theory of industrial district, the concept of the new industrial district has been under confusion and obscurely cited. Amid the confusion, it is possible to distinguish two major branches of the New Industrial District theories. One is Granovetter style theory of social relations & embeddedness that emphasize highly integrated and at the same time flexible social cohesion based on division of labor and trust. The other branch of theory comes from Michael Piore and Sabel's unique theorization (Piore & Sabel 1984). As will be discussed in chapter 3, the contribution of the theory is the new awareness of the importance of social fabric in economic & industrial performance.

As an extension from the "social fabric" notion, there has been another important avenue in understanding the relationship between the social component and economic performance. One of the frequently cited theorists has been Robert Putnam who has argued the importance of social capital, in contrast to the existing notion of capital in economic sense.

Civic Culture has been a major explanatory variable in persuading audience on the outcomes of a political system since the 1950s and 60s. On this foundation, what Putnam added was to link this prior foundation with his concept of "social capital" which he brings in from historical roots. The concept of social capital is Putnam's major determinant that produces divergence of institutional performance across southern and northern regional governments.

## Scope of the Book

Through chapter one, a prologue has been presented. From the existing approaches of globalization, it is not possible to find an industry level international comparative analysis to track the formation of economic blocs or globalization. Among diverse understandings of globalization, chapter two of this book has taken a notion that globalization is an integration process in which greater portion of world economy at macro and micro industry level is shaped & affected by several major economic indicators. The approach this book has adopted has revealed that in chapter, the U.S. money supply as a time series variable has been the most influential factor in shaping and thereby integrating the world economy.

The wage data utilized clearly, both in theoretical and mathematical senses, works as a proxy for profit, which can be understood as an industry performance indicator. The methodology of cluster analysis is, de facto, a way to approach a numerical taxonomy of the time series growth pattern of industries, while time series based discriminant analysis has been applied to find the influential determinant.

Part II of this book, from chapter 3 to 7, presents policy options in the contexts of globalization to promote the economy & industry. Chapter 3 has reviewed different, but related theoretical approaches to understand regional research clusters. Chapter 4 noted a micro level dynamic within the research clusters by analyzing the conditions & variables that would facilitate research networks. Chapter 5 has discussed electronics industry that developing countries and regions would regard as a knowledge intensive industrial sector. In chapter 6, a discussion was presented regarding public sector competitiveness with a special focus on social capital component. The last chapter 7 finally integrated and closed the discussion in this book by presenting the future directions of regional economic development with an implication for the role of the public and private sectors.

# 2

# International Comparison of Industry Performance

One of commonly shared idea among intellectual circles as well as lay persons since the later part of the 20<sup>th</sup> has been the increasing interactions among and between countries. Numerous different theories have tried to support their own arguments to explain the causes and consequences. Amidst these theories, one of the ideas to approach the increased interactions has been through the formation of economic blocs. Beyond the political boundary of economic blocs, there has been a long evolutionary trend of economic bloc formation, and this chapter is intended to decipher the dynamic of the economic blocs through wage data based analysis.

Analysis in this chapter will be started at aggregate international data to be followed by selected individual industry level data and analysis utilizing the data sets. The major focus of attempting a historical economic data to follow and track the economic bloc formation is to present the empirical side of the phenomenon. In some sense, what empirical data analysis can offer will open a way forum that different theories and disciplines can interact to understand the phenomenon of economic bloc formation.

The eventual aim, in this chapter, would be to investigate how different regions and industries in those regions have been affected in the formation of the global trend. In so doing, this chapter aims at finding out the major economic factors that affects the World Economy and selected individual industrial sectors and how the factors have shaped different industries and regions.

## Existing theories on Integration
### Economic Determinism : Interdependence and Transaction Costs

While a Marxist tradition argues that economic integration as a resolution to cope with contradictions of capitalist world(Cocks 1980), theorists in economic determinism or globalization show their intellectual tradition much closer to the neoclassical economic theory. It is this vein that the economic integration school finds that expansion of markets due from developments in science & technology and its application in communication & transportation as the major cause that brought economic integration.(Keohane & Nye 1977; Geoffrey 1998) In other words, changes in socio-economic backgrounds increased market size and interdependence among countries, which resulted in the formation of major economic blocs.

To the scholars, increased interdependence could be interpreted in terms of transaction costs (McKay 1996). When transaction costs are negligible, compared to gains from international transactions, it is natural to expand trade. If, however, transaction costs are substantial or distributed unequally among trading countries, it would be relatively small countries that would favor institutional framework to reduce vulnerability. Economic integration is considered as one of the institutional arrangement in this context. To elaborate the idea, the following can be suggested. Since the 1950s, according to economic determinism, the World economy has experienced structural changes. Especially, in Europe, individual countries has built a consensus that it would be in their interests to integrate in managing inflation and stability of currency.(Brummer 1993; Levi 1987) As a critique, economic determinism has its weakness in that it regards inter-relationship between economy and politics as a causal relationship. To establish a causal relationship, it is important to provide how the causal link can be established. Also, it is essential to show micro-economic or industry level evidence to support the dynamic of integration. Economic determinism lacks sufficient conditions to be a causal explanation and leaves much room for empirical works.

### Political Determinism

Political determinism, in contrast to economic determinism, emphasizes capacity and will of politics in forming economic integration. Among diverse views in this category, theorists in inter-governmentalism claims that participation into economic integration is determined by national interests and that national interests are defined by the position of a country in the international system (Waltz 1979). In comparison, another branch argues that national interests are defined by domestic politics (Bulmer 1983). These political explanations were not sufficient enough to persuade readers on how economic integration was accomplished. Intergovernmentalism assumes that government represents national interests on a monopolistic basis excluding societal influence. Therefore, if there is any possibility that Non-governmental organizations(NGOs) or interests in international arena can be established, monopolistic position of the government would be reduced. In contrast, theorists of domestic politics are not free from critiques, since domestic politics was regarded as a reflection of domestic industrial and economic interests and thereby repeating the logic of economic determinism.

As shown above, existing literature has discussed on how economic integration was brought about from economic and political contexts. What is lacking in these traditions is more empirically founded research that would provide support for their arguments. Furthermore, an empirically based research in itself finds room for its own appeal when it can present a spectrum of different industrial and interests gaining and losing with the advent of economic integration. This paper, noting the necessity, tackles this point. Especially, this paper questions whether there has been a common economic dynamic that has driven the economic integration. Also, this research presents a wider scope than the existing literature in the sense that countries included range from European to Asian countries. If there is any common economic dynamic per se that has had major impact on globalization and integration, this paper can present how different industrial sectors of different regions are affected, and thereby provide clues to fill the gaps in the existing theories.

## Research Scope and Methodology

### Data source

In this research, data used for analysis is the Bureau of Labor Statistics(BLS) of the U.S. Government in time-series cross national format between 1985 and 2001. In this data set, this research selected several key industrial sectors appropriate for international comparison. While there are benefits to include large number of industries in analysis, this paper restricted numbers of industries with reasonable grounds. Instead, this research tried to increase the number of countries as long as the countries have comparable industry data in time series format. Selecting industrial sectors was performed by choosing sectors classified by the U.S. Standard Industrial Classification (SIC) codes. There-fore, it was possible to distinguish big chunks of industrial sectors and their sub-divisions. With the "big" structure, it was expected that by choosing small number of representative industrial sectors, empirical tracking of economic integration would be possible.

In selecting the sectors, several factors are considered. First, selection was made among sectors that produce major industrial products and thereby have major impacts on the economy. Sectors such as automobile and industrial machinery were the examples. Second, a balance between heavy and light industrial sectors was considered. Textile industry was selected to reflect this factor. Indeed, industrial sector like Textile offers good data availability as well, since almost every country has the industry. Third, reflecting its impor-tance, electronics sector was included. Fourth, data availability was one of the most crucial factors in deciding the sectors. When certain sector became unavailable due to large portion of missing data in major countries, this research took the nearest US SIC codes to find its closest relative. With the above criteria, seven industrial sectors are selected: auto, textile, fabricated metal & machinery, industrial machinery, shipbuilding & repair, electronics, and primary metal products.

## Methodology used in research

Research method used in this analysis is designed to extract and discover his-torical change of industrial performance recorded in historical wage data. Eco-nomics literature has provided with theoretical basis for using wage as the performance measure with a notion of labor rent (Blanchflower 1996; Katz and Summers 1989). After theoretical foundation has set up, empirical research to apply the concept in historical & industrial setting has developed. Researches on U.S. industrial performance during the New Deal era(Ferguson and Galbraith 1997) and U.S. industrial performance since 1970s on (Gal-braith and Calmon 1996) show how wage analysis can contribute to the understanding of economic history driven by economic forces including "tech-nological change". Outside the U.S. case, researches on Korea (Kim, J 1997, Galbraith & Kim 1998) presented how wage analysis can work as a policy evaluation methodology in interpreting major determinants from the analysis.

What is common from these researches is the notion that historical wage data records the dynamic of an economy. To extract the dynamic of an econ-omy, this research employs two steps of methods: cluster and discriminant analysis. With cluster analysis, this research intends to extract an evolution-like track of how an economy has changed. If units under study are industries, then the cluster analysis would provide an industrial history of a country. It is this context that cluster analysis has been used in researches performed in OECD countries in identifying technology & knowledge flow in industrial development and scientific & technological proximity of industrial activities.(OECD 1997) Clustering is performed on the basis of yearly wage change rates of each unit. Cluster analysis provides a grouping structure which is formed by the Ward's method(Ward 1963) that maximizes between group variance and minimizes within group variance. [1]

Then, the next step was to use discriminant analysis to extract the determinants that resulted in the grouping structure yielded from cluster analysis (Galbraith & Kim 1998; Slottje et. al. 1991). Interpreting how each unit(e.g. industry) has performed under the determinants extracted allows us to understand how and to what degrees the history of industries has been affected.[2] Succeeding the research tradition, this research takes a bold step in the sense that this research took nations as the unit for cluster and discriminant analysis. The underlying notion is that if the methodology has proven to be useful in each country's industrial history, it would be reasonable to expect that the identical methodology can be applied in studying the historical formation and the evolution of major economic blocs, as long as data availability permits. With this aim, cluster and discriminant analysis were employed to conduct the wage analysis.

## Research Findings

### *Tracking Major Economic Blocs at Aggregate Level*

With cluster analysis, this research tried to find the existence of major economic blocs through empirical tracking of wage data. In doing so, a two stage approach, one at aggregate and the other at industry level, was used. First, a cluster analysis at an aggregate level with all manufacturing industries of 29 countries from 1985 to 1994 and of 27 countries from 1985-2001 were

---

1.  For mathematical expression for cluster analysis, refer to Appendix of this book.
2.  Formal expression for using discriminant analysis can be found in the Appendix of this book.

attempted. The reason for doing the second attempt was to keep up with the major data set using 1985-1994 data in this research. Due to data availability at industry level and wider scope to include different regions to test economic bloc formation, this research tried to maintain 27 countries, while eliminating the ones with data problems in the extended analysis.

## *Aggregate Level Clustering*

In both cases, covering between 1985 and 1994 and between 1985 and 2001, this research reports historical formation of major economic blocs as shown in (Figure 2-1 and 2-4). It is possible to distinguish two major groups: one on the left hand side and the other on the right hand side.

Looking at member countries in the left hand side group suggests the name of the group. The left hand side group is a concentration of European countries, and thereby called the European Union concentration Group. Similarly, the right hand side group features Asian countries and NAFTA countries. More interesting point is that within the right hand side group, there is a clear sub-division of Asian country group(Taiwan, Korea, Hong Kong, and Singapore) and NAFTA country concentration group(US, Mexico, Canada). One finds Australia and Sri Lanka as member of the NAFTA concentration group. It is still possible, however, to call this group as NAFTA-Pacific group, with an exception of Sri Lanka.

Looking at the 1985-2001 cluster tree diagram (figure 2-4), it is possible to find similarities & differences. In figures 2-2 and 2-3, it is possible to distinguish two major groups: European group and the Pan-Pacific group. Within the European group, it is feasible to sub-divide the group into Europe I and II. In Europe I group, countries ranging from France, Germany mainly located in central Europe are included. In comparison, in Europe II group, countries in the North-West and South West of Europe are included. Regarding differences, followings can be presented. First, among NAFTA group countries, Mexico became an outlier within the boundary of the Pan-Pacific-NAFTA group. Second, within Pan-Pacific group, Singapore and Hong Kong have moved from a sub-group with Korea to the NAFTA group. Third, countries like New Zealand and Australia joined the Pan-Pacific group from the European group in the previous period. Fourth, Japan, previously located in the European group in 1985-1994 analysis has found its new position near Korea. Regarding similarities, European countries, in general, showed relative stableness in their clustering pattern in two data periods. Yet, in the previous period, it was possible to find a three sub-group structure within the European group, while in the 1985-2001 data period, a two group structure became evident, as shown in Figure 2-4.

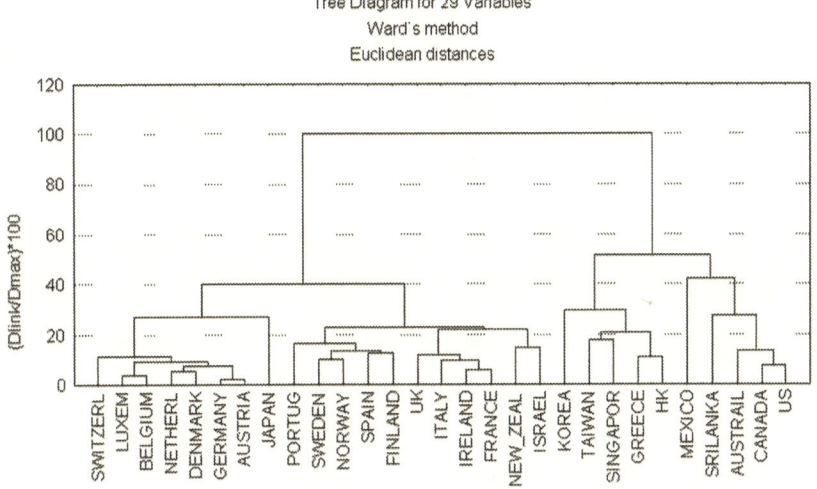

Figure 2-1: Cluster Result of Economic Integration (1985-1994)

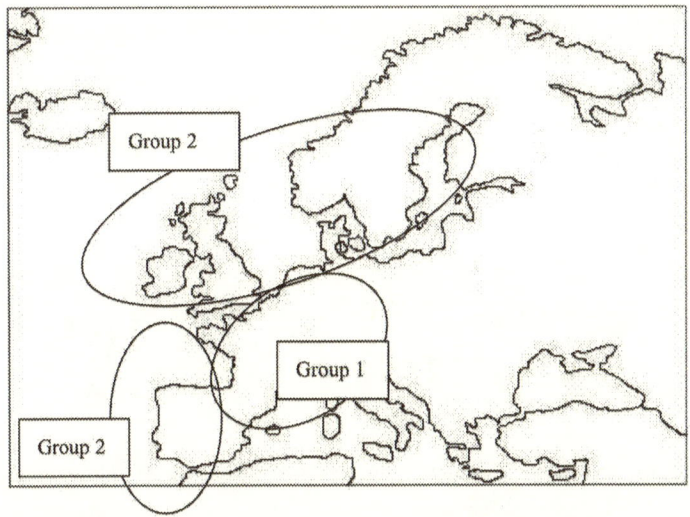

Figure 2-2 A Two Group Structure within the European Group

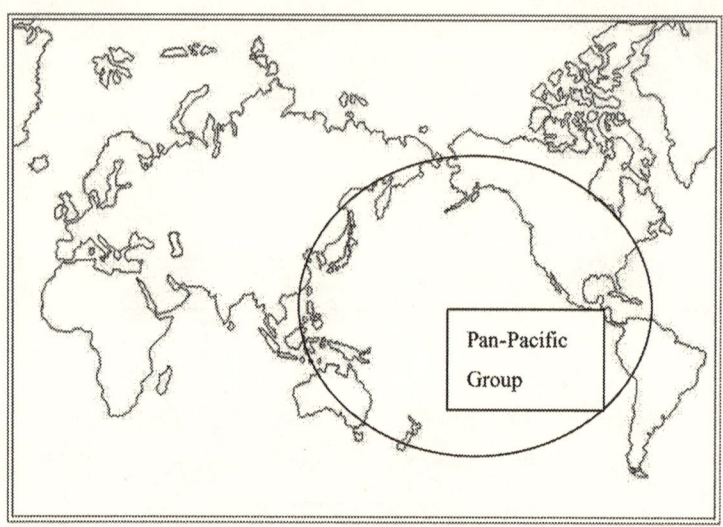

Figure 2-3 The Pan-Pacific Group

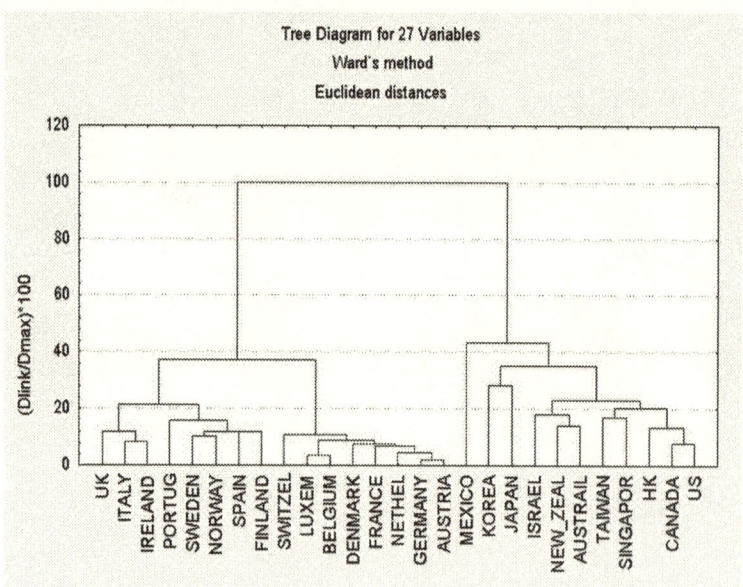

Figure 2-4: Cluster Result of Economic Integration (1985-2001)

## *Aggregate Level Determinant of Economic Blocs*

Then a question follows: what is the economic dynamic that has shaped the formation of economic bloc found from the analysis of empirical wage data? As discussed in the preceding section, historical economic data, in general, and wage data specifically, records economic history. Therefore, finding out the dynamic allows researchers to further understand the phenomenon under study. In this research, with the help of discriminant analysis which enables linear decomposition of time series data, the major impetus was found. The U.S. money supply(money supply plus quasi money supply) explains 86%(in the data set for 1985-1994), and 88% (in the data set for 1976-1996[3]) of total wage variation at aggregate level international analysis. In the analysis with extended data period, also the US money supply pattern was discovered to be the determinant in shaping the global level trend by explaining 100% of total wage variation at the aggregate level. As mentioned in chapter 1 as the focus of the book, given the U.S. money supply pattern as the aggregate level determinant, what would be drawing attention is to find whether the U.S. money supply would be extracted in the cases of individual selected industrial sectors as the determinant of industrial performance and thereby reveal the formation of economic blocs. If the existence of the economic blocs can be confirmed, then with discriminant analysis, an analysis will be followed to present which country or which group has been relatively benefited from the movement of the U.S. money supply, if it is found to be the most influential one.

## *Tracing Economic blocs at Industry Level*

Textile Industry

Textile industry is an ubiquitous industrial sector, which is translated into a possibility of generating internationally comparable data. In this research, textile industry was narrowed down to US. SIC 22,23, and 31, which represent core manufacturing in the industry. Figure 2-5 shows a clear picture of three major groups being formed over the period between 1985 and 1994. From left to right, one finds two European groups and NAFTA-Pacific group on the right hand side.

---

3. To extend data period up to 1970s, averaging the missing data may be needed for industry level analysis. With this reason, this research strictly limited the data period from 1985-2001.

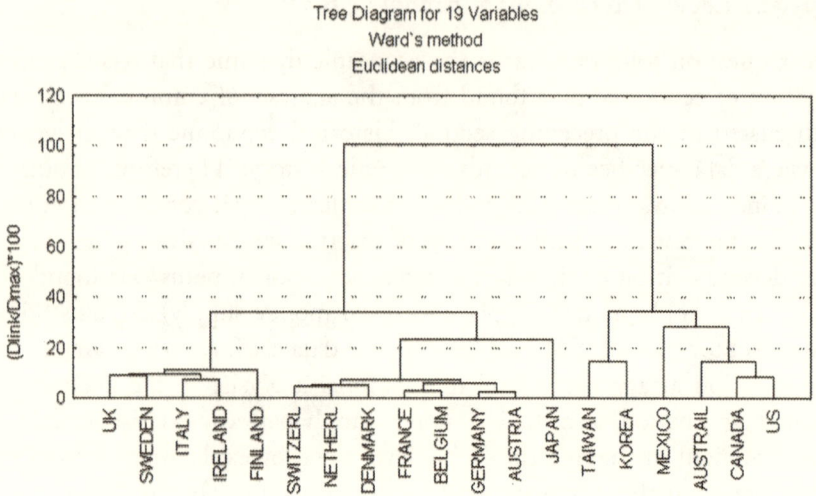

Figure 2-5: Cluster Result for Textile Industry (1985-1994)

Textile is such a ubiquitous industry. From the early stages of industrialization to the later advanced economic stages, it is feasible to expect that the sector would remain in a country with critically different contents or portfolios for its survival. From figure 2-6, it is quite clear that the NAFTA/Asian countries are involved in a relatively lower strata of textile market, in comparison to such European groups that include Italy and U.K.

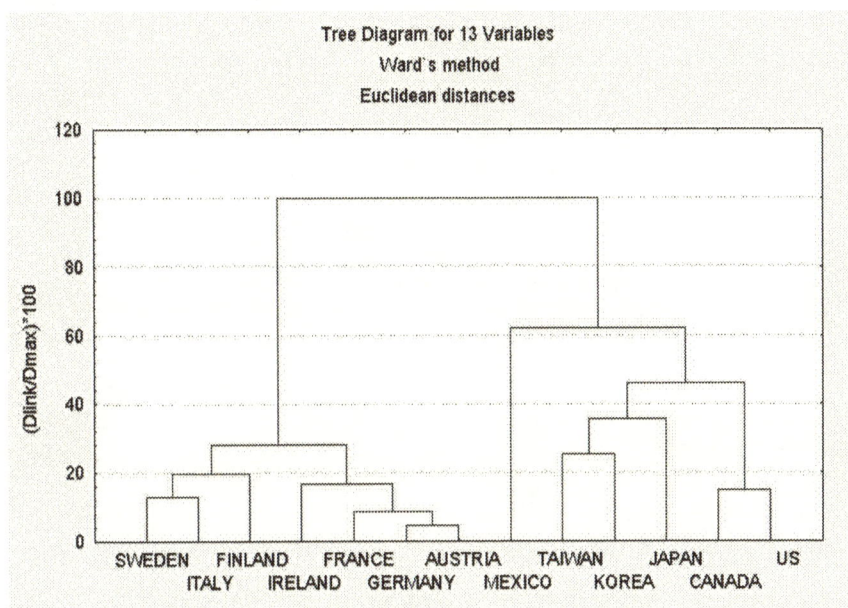

Figure 2-6: Cluster Result for Textile Industry (1985-2001)

From the cluster analysis of 1985-2001 data period, it is possible to confirm the pattern found from the aggregate level analysis. One can find that NAFTA and European groups, while within the European group, there is a sub-division between Europe 1 and 2 as explained at the aggregate level. Japan, previously located within the European group in 1985-1994 analysis is now located in the Pan-Pacific group.

With discriminant analysis, canonical roots are found. Among them, the first root, the U.S. money supply, takes about 80% of total wage variation across textile industries surveyed. Looking at individual countries and their performance under the U.S. money root expressed in scores found that NAFTA and Pacific countries were benefited with the movement of the first root, the U.S. money supply (Figure 2-8). This can be interpreted in the following way; Textile industries in these countries have been closely tied to the U.S market.(Murphy 1995; Fuentes 1993) This means that their performance or sales volume is linked to U.S. domestic economy or more specifically consumer demands for their products. Under this circumstance, it is possible to infer that it has been the money supply that has affected consumer demands.

From a discriminant analysis from 1990-2000 period, identical to the previous period, the U.S. Money supply expressed in M2 was the determinant of wage performance. The U.S. money root explains nearly 100% of total variation, since the two group structure has produced the single root. Comparing the result with the outcome of the previous period reports that NAFTA and Pacific countries were benefited

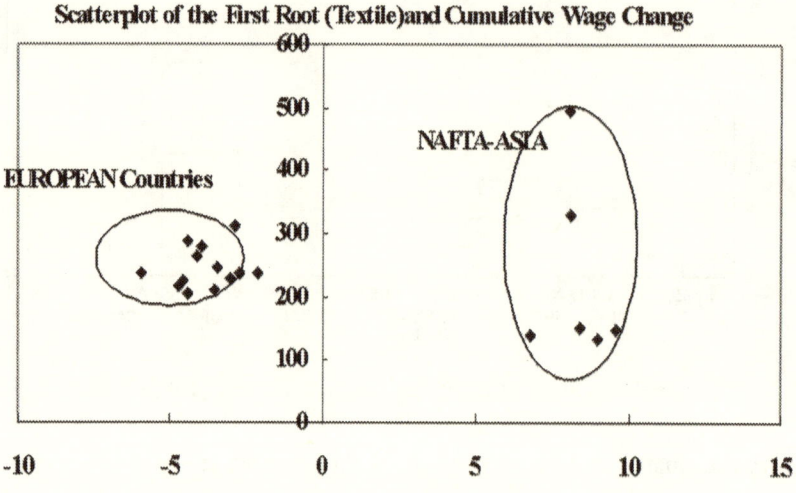

Figure 2-8: Industry Performance (Textile Industry) (1985-1994)

With the movement of the U.S. money supply has not been changed, only difference that can be found is that regarding the impact from the U.S. money supply root, there is a clear sign of convergence in the degrees of benefits that countries could get. This is indicated by narrower band of dots (countries) in figure by being concentrated near score 10 on the horizontal axis of the root.

Regarding the location of the European countries, it is noteworthy that their relatively disadvantageous position has not been changed in both time periods of 1985-1994 and 1990-2000. Interpretations on the country behavior would be virtually identical to those from the 1985-1994 period.

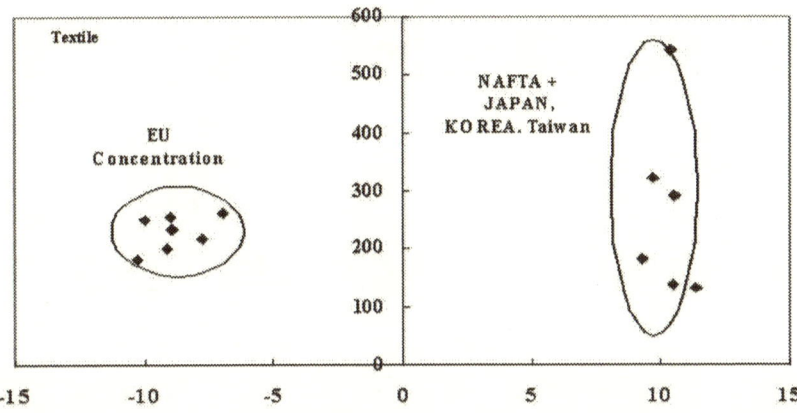

Figure 2-9: Industry Performance by economic groups (Textile Industry)
(1990-2000)

Auto Industry

Auto Industry is one of the key industries where heavy industrialization has taken place. In this analysis, the U.S. SIC 371was used to define auto industry. In Figure 2-10, one finds four distinct groups of auto producing countries. From left, there are two European groups, while there are two groups on the right hand side: Japan-Korea-Taiwan group and NAFTA groups.

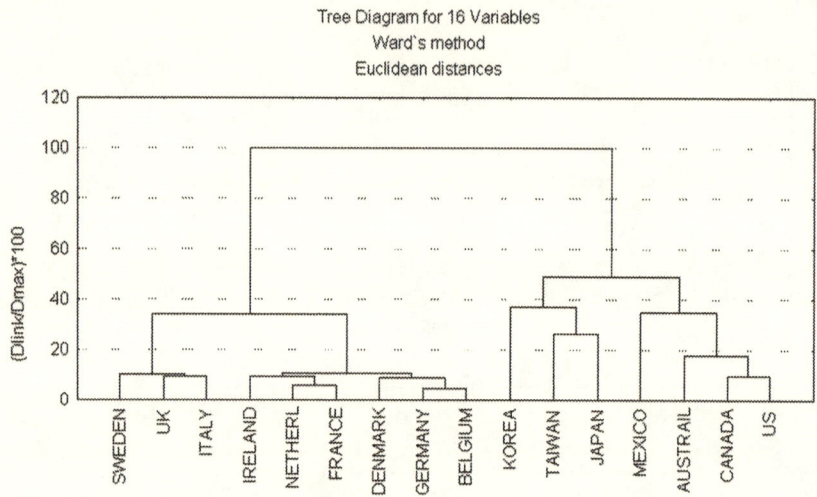

Figure 2-10: Cluster Result for Auto Industry (1985-1994)

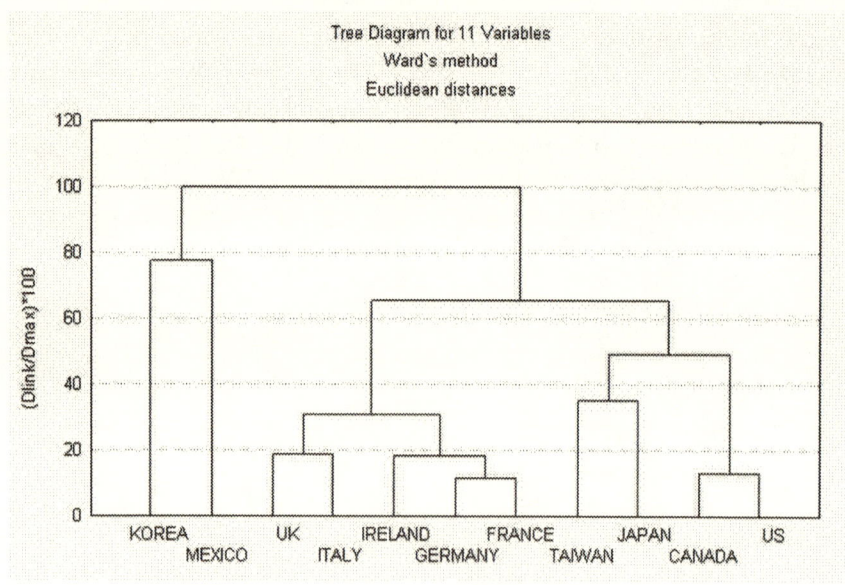

Figure 2-11: Cluster Result for Auto Industry (1985-2001)

From a cluster analysis of 1985-2001 period of wages in auto industry of selected countries, it is possible to point out at lest two points of interests from the previous attempt of international industrial clustering. First, Korea and Mexico, that were in the Pan-Pacific/NAFTA group in 1985-1994 analysis, have been relocated themselves by forming a third independent group. This reflects the behavior of the respective industry in those countries in international business. Second, except for Ireland, the sub-division of Europe 1 and 2 groups were relatively well preserved in the later analysis, which verify the stout grouping structure.

What is conspicuous with auto industry was that,among the roots found in discriminant analysis, the first root was not related to the U.S. money supply pattern at all. The U.S. money supply was best matched with the second root of auto industry's wage change pattern. The second root took about 24.6% of total variation in wage performance of auto industries in the international data set under research. This suggests that performance of auto industry may be affected more by other factors. In other words, trade volume of automobiles is smaller when compared with domestic consumption of the product.(O'Loughlin & Anselin 1996; Kahler 1995; Emmerij 1992) With this root, auto industries in Korea, Japan, and Taiwan were benefited most with respect to the U.S. money supply change (Figure 2-13 and 2-14). Despite the advantage, however, only 24% of total wage variation is related to the second root.

Discriminant analysis with 1992-2000 period reports that U.S. money supply as the major economic determinant of the international wage variation for selected countries in this industrial sector by explaining about 99 % of total international wage variation in the data period. This is a sharp departure vis-à-vis the finding from the earlier period. Judging from the result from the previous period, it has been possible that the auto industry can be a sole example that globalization of economic bloc formation either would not work or delayed for a substantially prolonged period. Looking at the new finding from the extended period, at least, hints that something has occurred during the 1990s in the world auto industry. In this research, it is assumed that global "earthquake" of merger & acquisition cases in auto industry has prompted the formation of economic blocs in auto industry (see Table 2-5 in Chapter Appendix). In the previous case, a possible implication would have been that auto industry can be recorded as a show case, in which national industrial policy can work against the global trend of economic bloc formation. With the finding from the later period, however, the possible implication has been faded away.

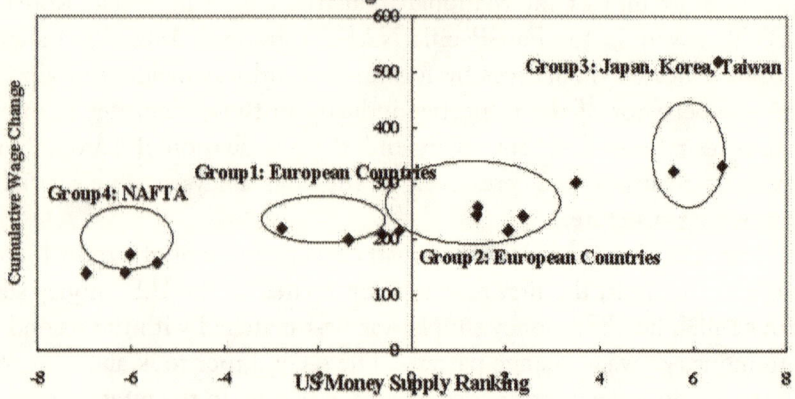

Figure 2-13: Industry Performance by Economic Groups (Auto Industry)
(1985-1994)

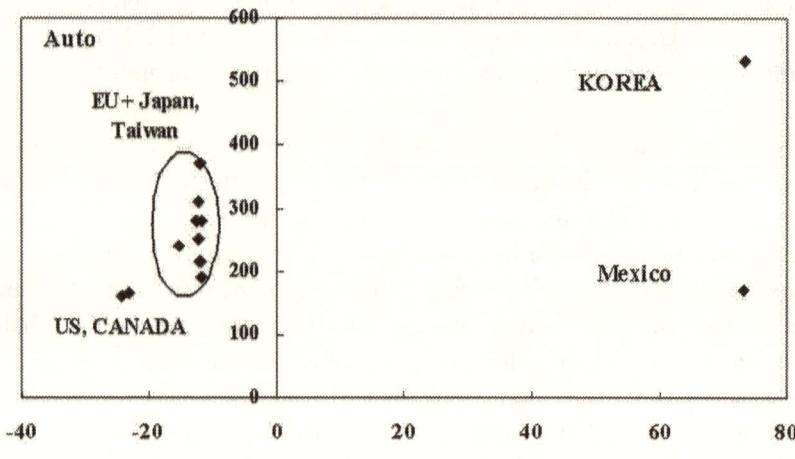

Figure 2-14: Industry Performance by Economic Groups (Auto Industry)
(1992-2000)

Compared to the previous period of 1985-1994, in the period between 1992-2000, discriminant analysis presents another important distinction.

That is, in the latter data period, the number of countries that have been benefited by the U.S. Money supply (M2) has been reduced. In figure, those benefited nations included Japan, Korea, Taiwan and even some of the European countries located in the positive ranking area on the horizontal axis. In 1992-2000 period, the only benefited nations have shrunken to Mexico and Korea, which suggests that these countries may have enjoyed particularly "favored" access to the U.S. and other international markets. In the Mexican case, it would be a NAFTA factor, while in the Korean case, it can be evidenced by the statistics of export increase of the sector. In the Korean case, it would b reasonable to infer that specific industry dynamic, including trade structure & parts supply chains, and economic structure, including exchange ratio and capital supply, have been so conditioned in a way to be benefited from the U.S. Money supply. This, in other way however, would work as a critical hazard factor for the industry when conditions are unfavorably conditioned.

Second, from the discriminant analysis, most European countries are located to represent relatively disadvantageous position with the movement of the U.S. money supply. Countries like Taiwan and Japan that have traditionally benefited from the U.S. money supply factor are also located close to the European nations. Third, among European nations, it is quite clear that they form a unified group in figure 2-14.

**Table 2-1 World Automobile production (in million units)** *

| Y93 | 13.1 | 2.8 | 13.1 | 2.3 | 11 | 3.5 | 0.6 |
| Y94 | 14.5 | 3.1 | 14.6 | 1.8 | 11 | 4.1 | 0.66 |
| Y95 | 14.3 | 2.8 | 14.5 | 2 | 10 | 4.5 | 0.62 |
| Y97 | 15.6 | 2.7 | 14.7 | 1.4 | 11 | 5.7 | 0.42 |
| Y98 | 15.5 | 2.25 | 15.8 | 1.6 | 9.6 | 4.15 | 0.38 |
| Y99 | 17.6 | 1.7 | 16.94 | 2.9 | 9.8 | 7 | 0.414 |
| Y00 | 17.67 | 2.14 | 16.92 | 3 | 10 | 7.98 | 0.429 |
| Y01 | 15.5 | 2.22 | 17 | 2.4 | 9.8 | 8.35 | 0.76 |

* Source: Korea Asso. of Automobile Industry, Statistics, each year
Production volume of automobile industry by region can be presented as in Table 2–1 as a supporting data for the discussion of auto industry.

## Fabricated Metal & Machinery Industry

This industrial sector represents a backbone of one country's manufacturing capability at least in metal related hardware sense. In this category, U.S. SIC 34 through 38 are used to define the sector. In figure 6, one finds a three-group clustering structure of countries. At the left is the European group 1 which is composed of Norway, UK, Sweden, Italy, and Finland. In the middle, one finds European group 2 with Japan added to the group. On the right side is the NAFTA plus Taiwan and Korea, the two industrializing countries of Far East Asia. (Emmerij 1992)

From a cluster analysis with the extended 1985-2001 period, it is possible to glean three points of interests. First, Japan, previously located in the European countries group, has moved to the Pan-Pacific group. Second, within the European group, sub-groups of Europe I and II were maintained, while among countries in the Europe II, Norway and Ireland, have moved to group I. Third, inside the Pan-Pacific group, it is possible, in the case of Fabricated Metal & Machinery Industry sector, a specific division between NAFTA and the Asian groups was visible.

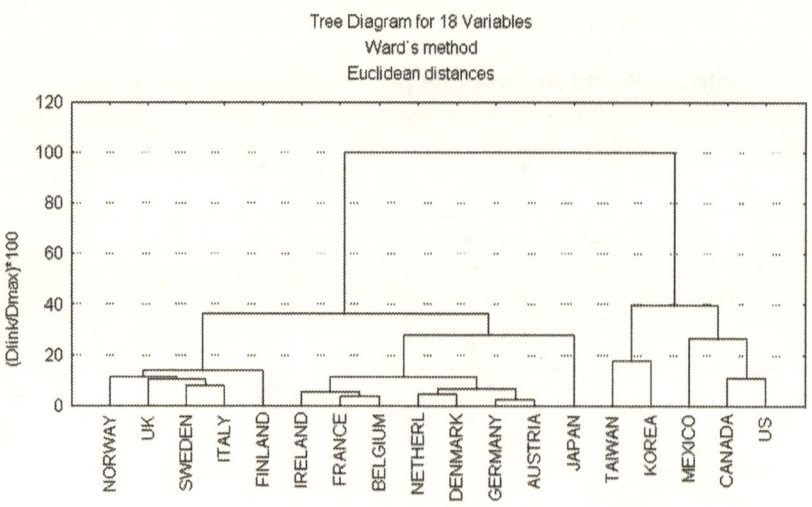

Figure 2-15: Cluster Result for Fabricated Metal & Machinery Industry (1985-1994)

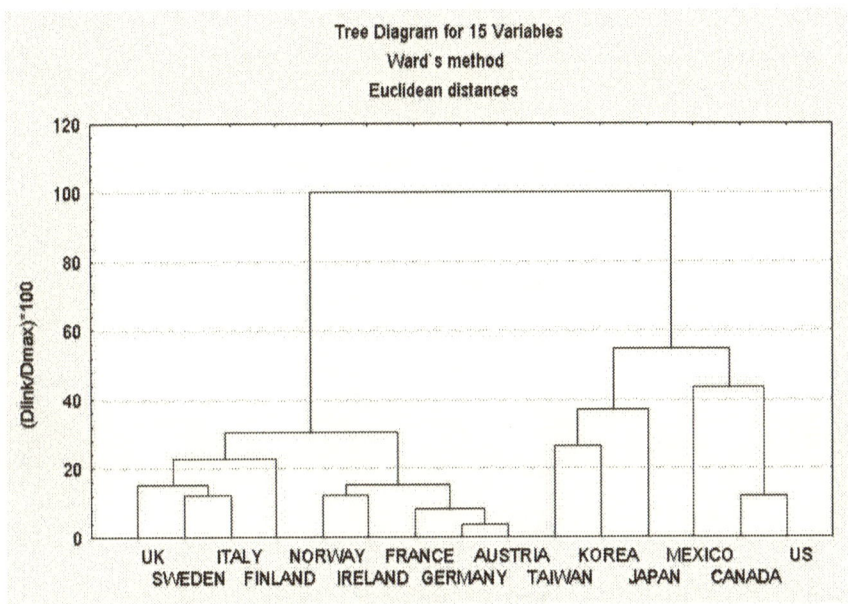

Figure 2-16: Cluster Result for Fabricated Metal & Machinery Industry (1985-2001)

With Discriminant analysis, this chapter reports that U.S. money supply as the major economic determinant of the international wage variation for selected countries in this industrial sector. One noteworthy point is that among the two roots acquired from discriminant analysis, 97% of total wage variation is related to the U.S. money supply. With the potent determinant, as shown in Figure 2-18, NAFTA countries including the U.S. and Korea, Taiwan were benefited with the movement of U.S. money supply. European countries in group 1 and 2 are relatively disadvantaged on the U.S. money supply root.

Discriminant analysis with 1991-2000 period reports that U.S. money supply as the major economic determinant of the international wage variation for selected countries in this industrial sector by explaining 100% of total international wage variation in the data period, due to the two group structure that yielded a single root. Discriminant analysis of 1991-2000 period for the Fabricated Metal & Machinery sector added several more findings. First, European countries became the beneficiaries of the U.S. money supply(M2). Second, in contrast, the number of Pan-Pacific group countries that have been benefited has decreased to only two countries, Taiwan and Korea respectively.

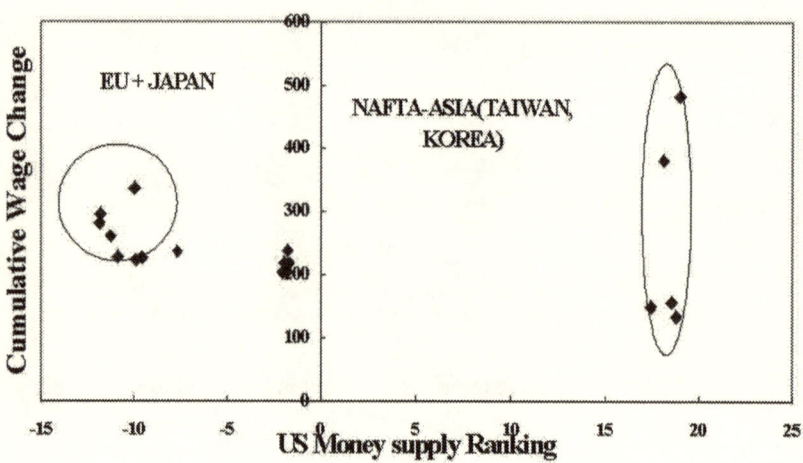

Figure 2-18: Industry Performance by Economic Groups (Fabricated Metal & Machinery) (1985-1994)

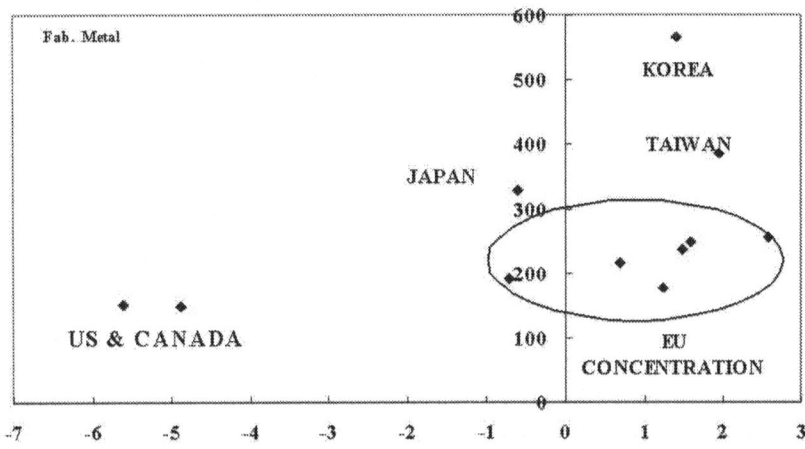

Figure 2-19: Industry Performance by Economic Groups (Fabricated Metal & Machinery) (1991-2000)

This implies the relative standing of the sector as an export industry in the two countries. As a supporting evidence, one of the information that could be utilized in analyzing industry characteristics would be trade structure. Table 2-2 shows the relative stance of major economic forces in their export performance.

## Table 2-2 Export Performance of General Machinery [*]

|       | EU   | US  | JAPAN |
|-------|------|-----|-------|
| Y90   | 644  | 288 | 303   |
| Y91   | 627  | 324 | 347   |
| Y92   | 637  | 322 | 352   |
| Y93   | 730  | 381 | 417   |
| Y94   | 801  | 420 | 466   |
| Y95   | 870  | 445 | 514   |
| Y96   | 993  | 497 | 505   |
| Y97   | 1087 | 631 | 543   |

**Table 2-2 Export Performance of General Machinery (Continued)**[*]

| Y98 | 1086 | 605 | 467 |
|-----|------|-----|-----|

* Source: EU Mechanical Engineering VDMA 2001. 3. (Unit: 100 million ECU)

## Industrial & Commercial Machinery Industry

The Industrial and Commercial industry sector is a value-added special machinery sector, which represents one country's industrial prowess. While the preceding fabricated metal and machinery sector encompassed a wide range of machinery and metal assembly producing sectors, this category narrowed its scope to the U.S. SIC 35 to contrast with the finding of the preceding section. In this industrial group, Figure 8 reports a two-group structure with Mexico being an outlier. The first group on the left hand side includes European countries such as Netherlands, Ireland, France, Switzerland, Denmark, Belgium, Germany, and Austria with an unique member, Japan. In comparison, the other group on the right side features U.S., Canada, and European countries like Sweden, Italy, Finland, U.K. Greece with Korea, Taiwan and Israel added. (Peak 1993)

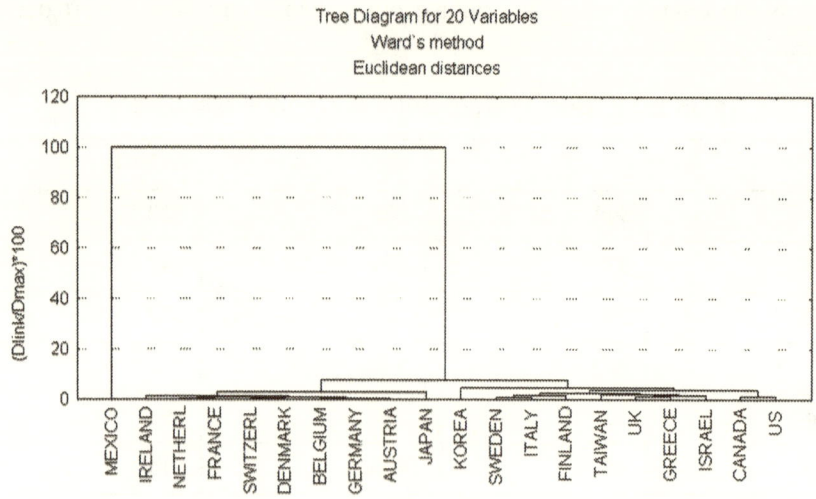

Figure 2-20: Cluster Result for Industrial & Commercial Machinery Industry (1985-1994)

Extended data period of 1985-2001 gave three additional findings to the existing body of knowledge. First, Japan joined the Pan-Pacific group by leaving the European group. Second, Korea and Mexico have formed an independent group, which hints their independent industrial performance, contrasted by other group countries. Third, the structure of Europe I and II has been preserved in Industrial & Commercial Machinery Industry case. The finding that Japan moved its affiliation was also found in aggregate level, textile, and fabricated metal product sectors, which strongly implicate that there has been a change in the "behavior" of the Japanese economy and industrial sectors as well.

Another observation to discuss comes from the clear "resolution" of the cluster structure. With the adding of years, cluster structure of the Industrial & Commercial Machinery Industry showed a better distinguished tree diagrams. In contrast to the tree diagram from the 1985-1994 period showed a relatively compressed distance among groups, while maintaining the group identity, the later tree diagram clearly showed a more developed group structure.

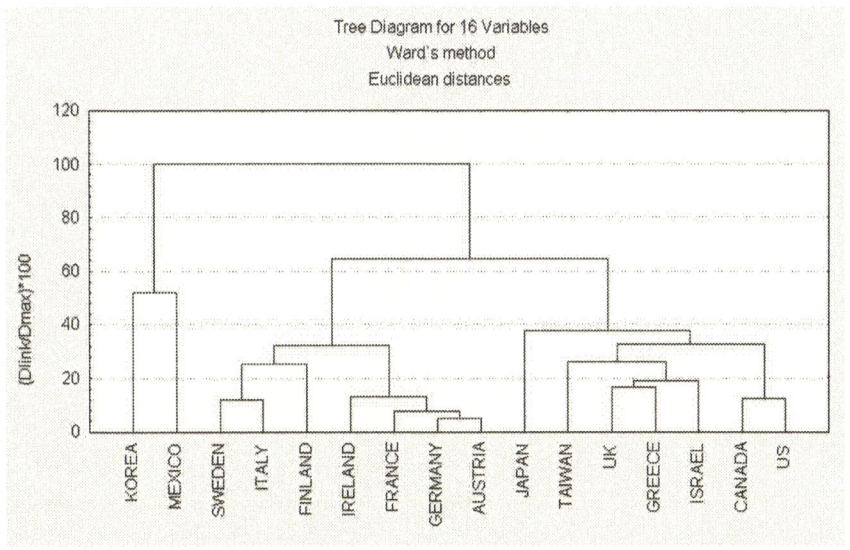

Figure 2-21: Cluster Result for Industrial Machinery Industry (1985-2001)

Interestingly enough, the two group structure yields a sole root in the discriminant analysis, and this root moves in close tightness with the U.S. money supply changes. Then, a following curiosity is that which group would benefit from the U.S. money supply changes. Figure 2-24 presents that group 1, which was on the right side on Figure 2-23, had a cumulative advantage over the period under study. European countries and Japan in the group had a clear advantage. This is contrary to the findings from other industrial sectors in the sense that other sectors, in the preceding parts, showed the group with U.S.-NAFTA concentration and Asian countries were the major beneficiaries from the movement of U.S. money supply root. It is reasonable to infer from the finding that the industrial sector defined by the U.S SIC 35 is a technologically sophisticated sector in which certain European countries and Japan had a clear technological advantage. The fact, that Japan is included in the advantaged group, while U.S. is not, suggests a possibility that the sector is more related to civilian use technology.

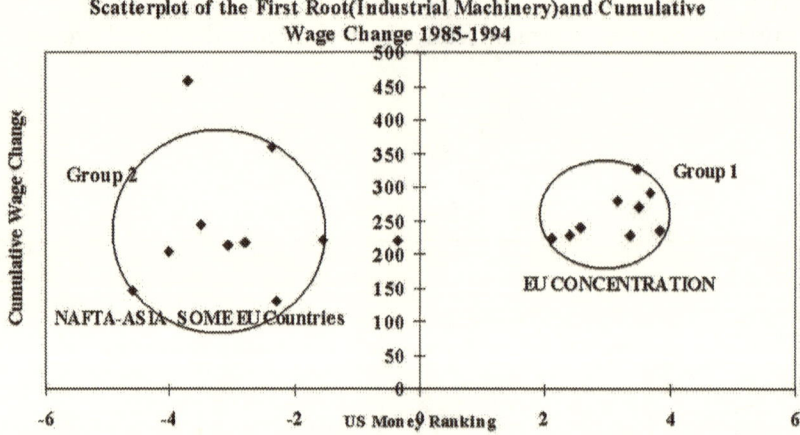

Figure 2-23: Industry Performance by Economic Groups (Industrial & Commercial Machinery industry) (1985-1994)

Discriminant analysis with 1989-2001 period reports that U.S. money supply as the major economic determinant of the international wage variation for selected countries in Industrial & Commercial Machinery sector by explaining about 97.7% of total international wage variation in the data period. Compared to previous period, the 1989-2001 data period offers some changes. First, While European countries maintained their status of the most benefited country group, the Pan-Pacific group countries have moved toward the right hand side, indicating that they also became beneficiaries of the U.S. Money supply root.

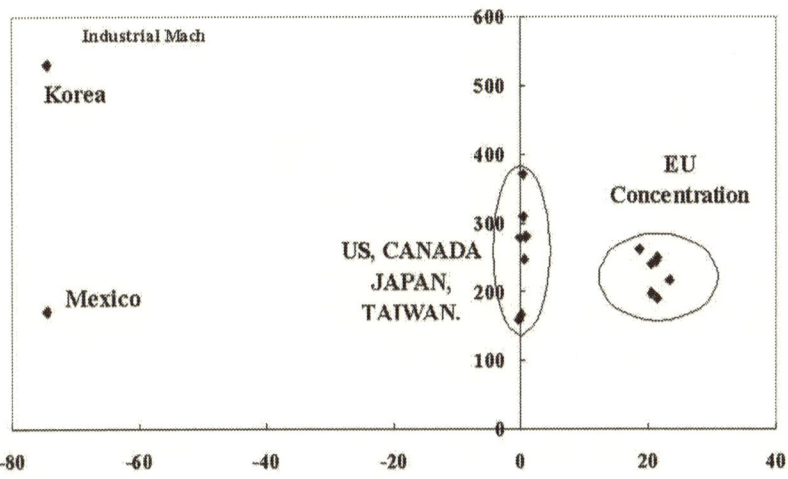

Figure 2-24: Industry Performance by Economic Groups (Industrial & Commercial Machinery industry) (1989-2001)

Second, in contrast to the general trend in the Pan-Pacific group, Korea and Mexico became outliers, showing that Industrial & Commercial Machinery industry in these two countries are not beneficiaries from the U.S. Money supply. This offers a hint to understand the uniqueness of the industry in the two countries. These two countries share a point that their industrial machinery products are not geared toward the movement of the U.S. economy. Indeed, most of Korea's heavy industrial export items have been exported to non-U.S. markets, mainly South and Southwest Asian countries. In Mexican case, the industrial sector is not a serious export industry, which may result in the location of the sector.

Shipbuilding and Repair

In shipbuilding &repair industry, there has been a trend of increasing competitiveness in Asian countries covering Japan, Korea, Taiwan, and China, which reflexively meant relative decline of the industry in European countries and in the U.S.(Lloyd's 1988 through 1997) To show industry structure and the determinant of industry structure, this section utilized the U.S. SIC 373 in defining the sector. Although China and Mexico were not included in the analysis due to data availability, this section provided an interesting spectrum of three groups in Figure 2-25. From left, group 1 covers U.K, Sweden, Italy, and Finland; group 2 includes Netherlands, Germany, Denmark, France, and Belgium; group 3 features Asian countries like Taiwan, Japan and Korea, U.S., Canada, and European countries like Portugal and Greece.

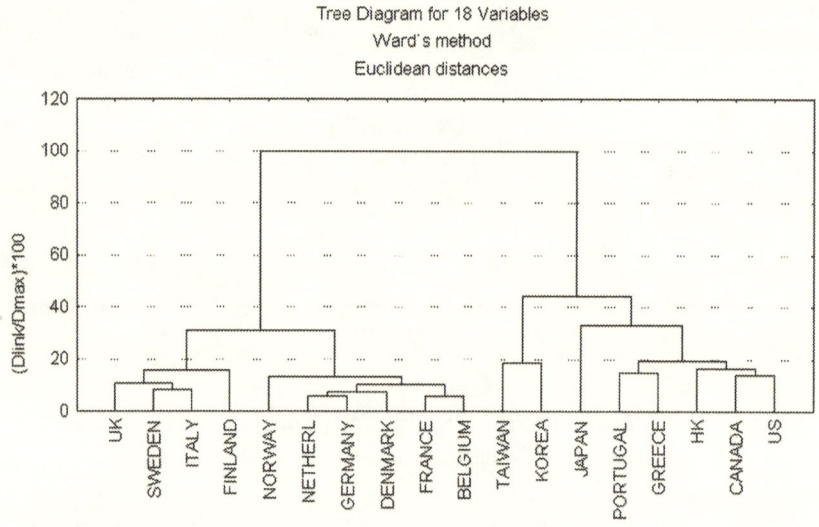

Figure 2-25: Cluster Result for Shipbuilding & Repair Industry (1985-1994)

Observing the cluster tree for the 1985-2001 period brings several points of interests. First, like in other industrial sectors, Japan has made an exodus from European country group into the Pan—Pacific group. Second, compared to most industrial sectors and aggregate level cluster trees, the distinction between Europe I and II is blurred in shipbuilding & repair sector case. Third, in contrast, like in other industrial sectors, within the Pan-Pacific group, a clear division between the Asian and the NAFTA groups was visible.

For this industry the three group structure results in two roots in the discriminant analysis. The first and the major root which covers about 80% of total wage variation in the Figure 2-27.

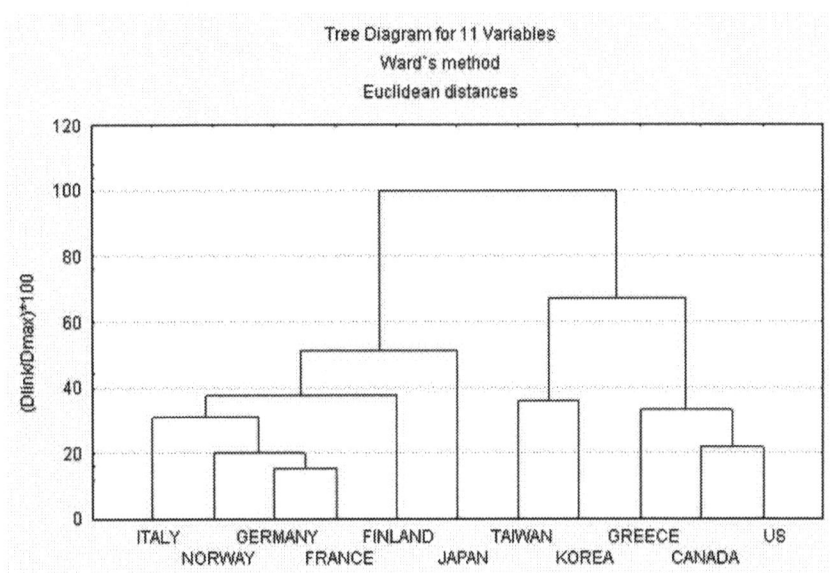

Figure 2-26: Cluster Result for Shipbuilding & Repair Industry (1985-2001)

For shipbuilding industry for the selected countries, the U.S. money supply was the major determinant.

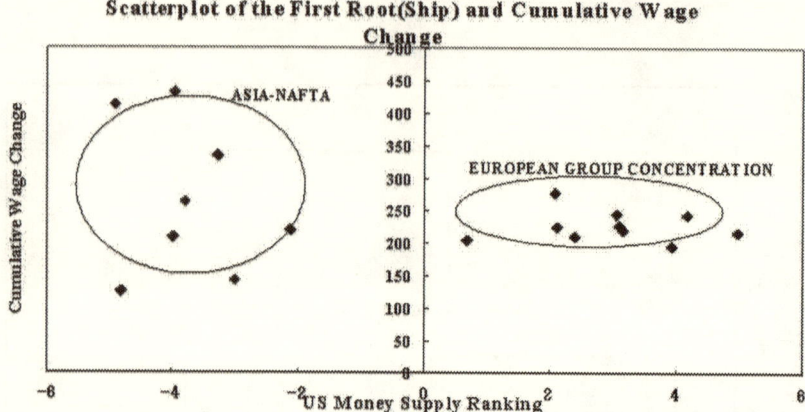

Figure 2-28: Industry Performance by Economic Groups (Shipbuilding &Repair Industry) (1985-1994)

Similar to the finding in the Figure 2-23 and 2-24, of the industrial & commercial machinery sector, it was found that U.S.—NAFTA and Asian countries were not benefited from the U.S. money supply movements, when compared to European countries (Figure 2-28). This finding suggests that competitiveness of the Asian shipbuilders come from a different source other than U.S. money supply changes.(O'Loughlin and Anselin 1996) Also this is a sharp contrast to textile and auto industry where industries in Asian countries were linked to the U.S. money supply. (Greenwood 1990).

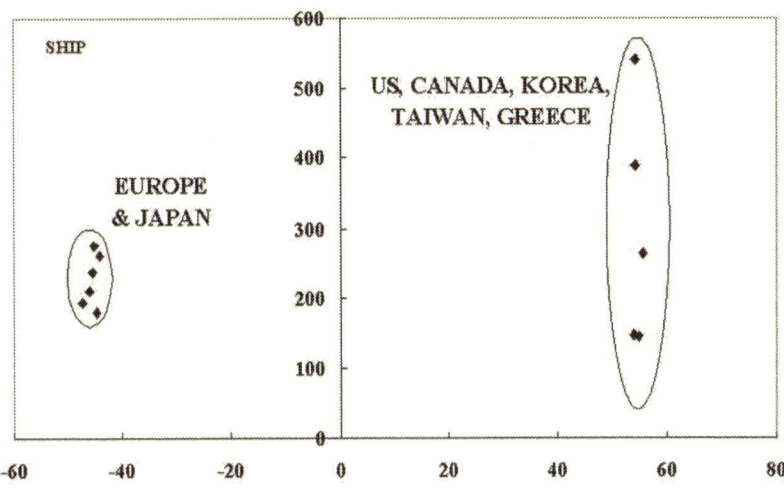

Figure 2-29: Industry Performance by Economic Groups(Shipbuilding & Repair Industry) (1992-2000)

Discriminant analysis with 1992-2000 period reports that U.S. money supply as the major economic determinant of the international wage variation for selected countries in Shipbuilding industry by explaining 100% of total international wage variation in the data period, due to the two group structure that yielded the sole root. Under the surface that the identical root of U.S. money supply root exists, there is a clear change in the members of benefited group countries. While European countries were in advantageous position in the 1985-1994 period, Europe and Japan have been relocated in the relatively disadvantageous area. This leaves the location of the Pan-Pacific group in the advantage zone in the right hand side in Figure 2-29. In some sense, this new figure reflects the reality of the shipbuilding industry better than the previous one. The reason for the argument comes from the fact that European ship yards mainly rely on value added, expensive ship orders, while Asian yards are closer to mass production style approach in the shipbuilding industry, although all shipbuilding process is based on batch production and not mass production based. In other words, the Pan-Pacific group countries can be understood to be "riding" the changes of world trade volume, signaled by the U.S. economic indicators like the money supply. Furthermore, the location of

European countries suggest the reasons why the countries have been requesting multi party negotiations among shipbuilders since the 1990s.

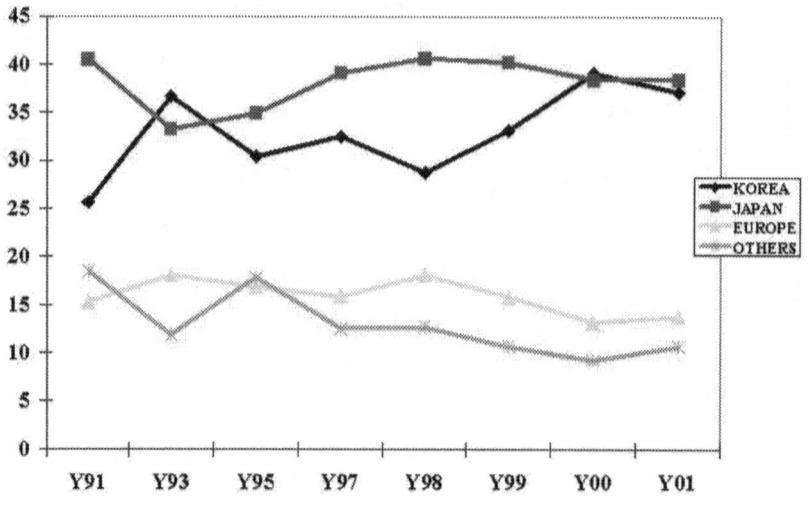

Figure 2-30 International Market Share of major Shipbuilding Nations
(New Ship building orders in Tonnage)
(Europe denotes Association of European Shipbuilders & Repairers.)
Data Source: Lloyd's World Shipbuilding Statistics, Each year
Re-calculated & processed for graphics

In a partial evidence & support to the explanations given in the preceding section, International Market Share of major Shipbuilding Nations can be presented, in which Japan, Korea, and China (included in others) are taking greater shares of world new shipbuilding. European builders have been concentrating on high end segments of the market. While presenting the figure, it is quite clear that the merits from the analysis adopted in this book can offer better understanding of the industry structure. In contrast to the relatively simple display of market shares, which is the most common way of expressing industry status, what has been presented in figure with the time series based discriminant analysis was the elative position and relative sensitivity of each shipbuilding nation against the major international economic indicator of the U.S. Money supply.

## Electronics Industry

In this industrial category, the U.S. SIC 36 was utilized. Electronics industry is a consumer driven industry, in which East Asian countries have shown dramatic increase in their competitiveness in the world market. In Figure 2-31, a three group structure was acquired from cluster analysis. Group 1 contains Asian countries like Korea, Taiwan, Hong Kong,and Mexico, another electronics producing country with Foreign Direct investments to the country. Group 2 includes European countries like Switzerland, Netherlands, Ireland, France, Belgium, Germany, and Austria with a single but powerful Asian country in electronics, Japan.(Ruhli et al. 1994) Countries in group 3 include Sweden, Italy, Finland, U.K. Greece and Israel and Canada as exceptions.

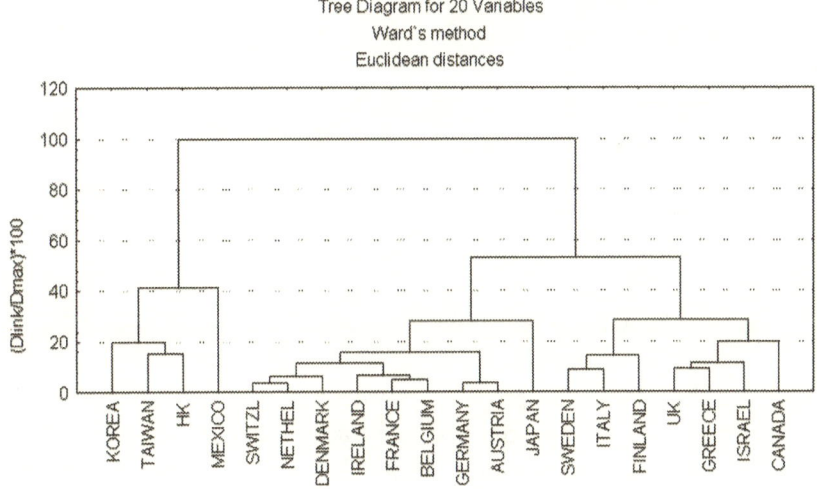

Figure 2-31: Cluster Result for Electronics Industry (1985-1994)

From the extended 1985-2001 cluster analysis (figure 2-32), it is possible to distinguish a three group structure. In the tree diagram, a group with Korea, Taiwan, Hong Kong, and Mexico is maintained; also common with the other industrial sectors, within the European country group, it was possible to subdivide the group into Europe I and II. Europe I group is mainly composed of the central continental European countries, while European II group contains Northern and South western European countries.

Comparing the two periods through which cluster analysis for the electronics sector was performed, similar to the cases of other industrial sectors, the cluster analysis with 1985-2001 data period offers a clearer definition of country groups.

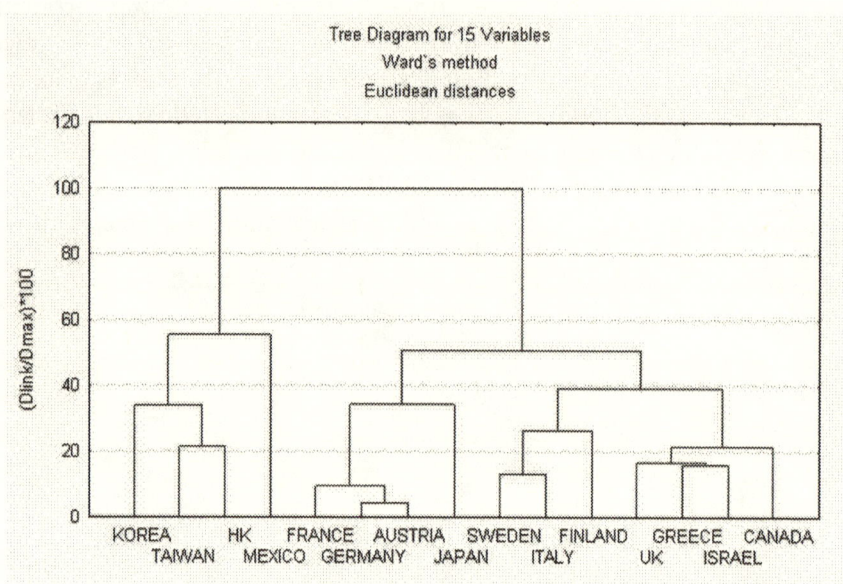

Figure 2-32: Cluster Result for Electronics Industry (1985-2001)

Discriminant analysis has provided two determinants of wage performance in the sector, among the two the first and the major root took nearly 86% of total variation of wage performance. Dovetailed with the other industrial sectors, the first root matched well with the U.S. money supply. To see the meaning of the first root, figure 2-34 and 2-35 present how different countries are affected. Quite opposite to the conventional belief, it was the European countries and Japan that were benefited by the changes in U.S. money supply. In comparison, Asian countries like Taiwan, Hong Kong, and Korea were relatively disadvantaged by the change of U.S. money supply. It is counter-intuitive in the sense that Taiwan, Korea, and Hong Kong were not benefited. A possible interpretation suggests that electronics sectors in Europe and Japan are keenly sensitive to U.S. Money supply, which affects consumer demand.(O'Loughlin & Anselin 1996; Kahler 1995) On the other hand, electronics products from Taiwan, Korea, and Hong Kong have been so low-priced to be necessities that change of U.S. of money supply does not work as the major determinant of industrial performance; and therefore wage performance of these electronics sectors does not reflect the impact of U.S. money supply as sharply as one would expect.

**Scatterplot of the First Root(Electronics Industry) and Cumulative Wage Change 1985-1994**

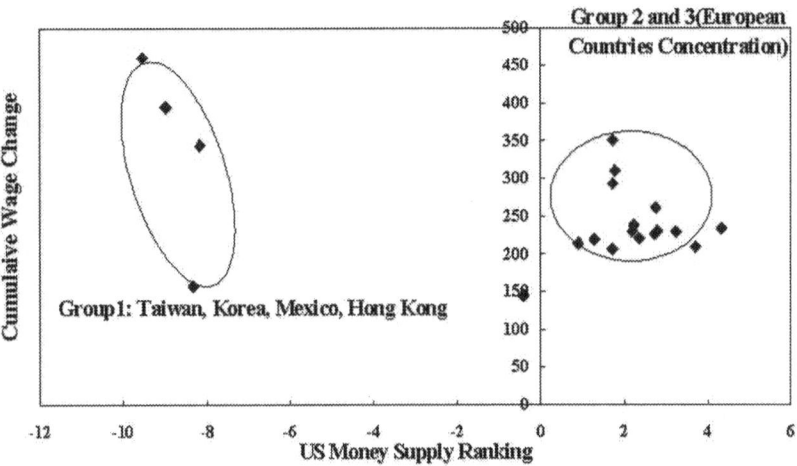

Figure 2-34: Industry Performance by Economic Groups (Electronics Industry) (1985-1994)

Discriminant analysis with 1990-2001 period reports that U.S. money supply as the second major economic determinant of the international wage variation for selected countries in electronics industry by explaining about 22.3% of total international wage variation in the data period. Compared to the findings from the figure 2-34 with the data period of 1985-1994, one can find, from figure 2-35 with the extended data period, a commonality and a difference as well. One peculiar commonality is the location of the Asian countries like Korea, Taiwan, and Hong Kong. Industrial performance of these countries have been unfavorably affected by the movement of the U.S. money supply change patterns. The interpretation for this seems to be unchanged from the one presented for the 1985-1994 analysis. For the Asian countries, electronics clearly has been one of the backbone export industries, exemplified by the export items such as semiconductors, PCs and major peripherals from Asia.

With this ground, it is quite likely that most analyst would think that electronics sector of these countries would be sensitive to the movement of the U.S. money supply.

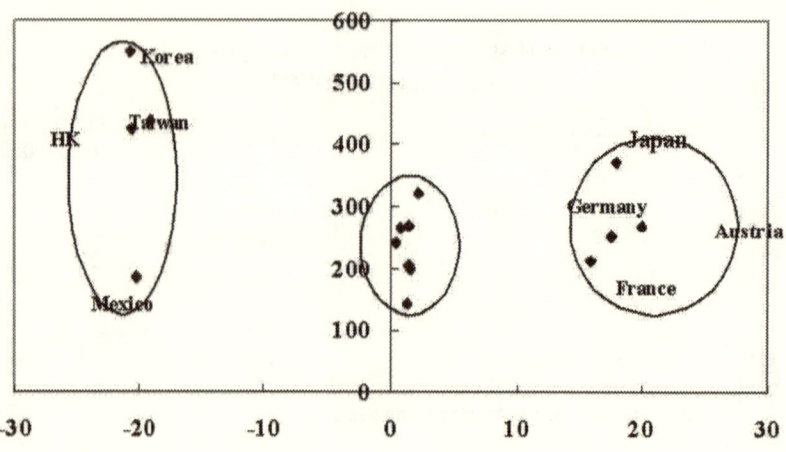

Figure 2-35: Industry Performance by Economic Groups (Electronics Industry) The Second Root Plotting (1990-2001)

Despite this possible conjecture, electronics sector of these countries were located in the left corner in figure 2-35. This seemingly anomalous phenomenon, however, finds an outlet when one thinks of the market strata of the major export electronics items coming from these countries., which have been mainly in entry market segments. This offers a clue in that the electronics products are, in fact, regarded as commodities consumption which are not affected greatly by the money supply. comes from the fact that the U.S. has imported, which has been conditioned by the demands from the U.S., which is pre-conditioned by the U.S. money supply. Regarding the difference, it is noteworthy that an European group concentration in the earlier period has faded away. From figure 2-35, countries in European group I and Japan are the most significantly benefited countries with the U.S money supply patterns.

## Primary Metal Products

Clustering result of primary metal industry from 1985 to 2001 period yielded a similar two group structure in which the Pan-Pacific and European groups exist. Within the European group, as seen in other industrial sectors, it was possible to distinguish group I and II. Based on industrial history of recent three or four decades, Asian countries have relied heavily on the U.S. market, and which is evidenced by the location of the countries in the cluster tree.

Despite this division, there is another dimension to understand the industry structure of this sector, which is related to types of products countries can produce. Asian countries, for example, until the 1990s, have focused on several relatively low–end market products with the advantages of the economies of scale. In contrast, European countries have accumulated experiences of producing specialty products, which clearly suggests that their industry behavior should be different from that of Asian countries. An answer to this question can come from the analysis of the discriminant root, the U.S. money supply. As seen in Figure 2-38, with the increase of the U.S. money supply, it has been the European countries that have been benefited. NAFTA plus Asian countries have been relatively under disadvantageous position.

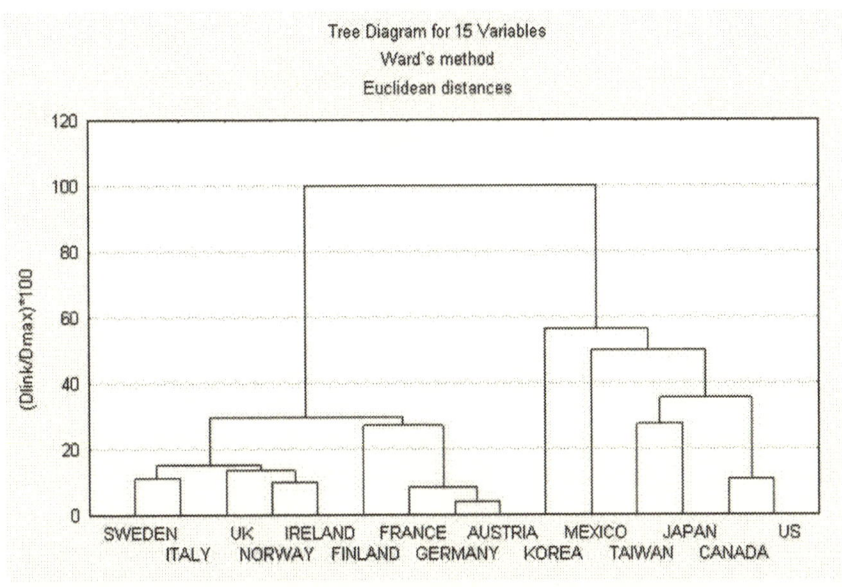

Figure 2-36 : Cluster Result for Primary Metal Industry (1985-2001)

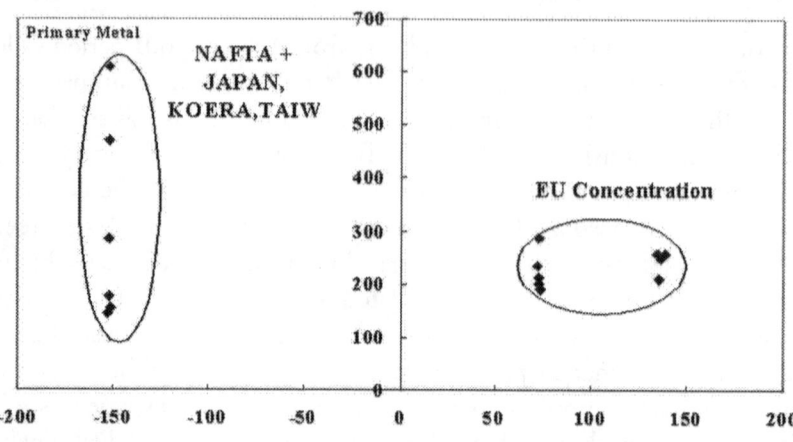

Figure 2-38 : Industry Performance by Economic Groups (Primary Metal)
(1990-2001)

It is noteworthy that within the NAFTA-Asian group, there exists a huge gap of cumulative wage increase, while in the European group, the gap is much smaller. Thus, it is possible to infer the followings. First, the degree that Asian countries have been affected by the U.S. money supply root is almost similar by their location over the-150 region, while the countries diverge greatly on the cumulative wage increase. In comparison, European countries shows a wage compression by being located between 200 to 300 % region on the vertical axis, the cumulative wage increase during the 1990-2001 period. Despite the compression and concentration of European countries, the degree that these countries have been affected by the U.S. money supply root shows a spectrum. This implies that there exists a special kind of metal products that have been favorably affected by the movement of the U.S. money supply.

## Summary

Preceding sections have reported an empirical tracking of several industrial sectors in historical formation of economics blocs. In presenting the results, two conspicuous findings can be mentioned. The first one is the existence of European group. It appeared either as one group or two sub groups. Similarly the NAFTA—Pacific group has shown its appearance. The second important finding was the impact of the U.S. money supply as the major determinant in forming the economic blocs and the development of the industries. A summary of findings can be presented in the following tables 2-3 and 2-4.

## Consequence of Globalization

As a concluding remark, the following points can be presented. First, an interesting question arose regarding the meaning and consequence of globalization. Would globalization mean homogenization? On this question, this research provided a fairly sophisticated answer. Globalization has led to two aspects of consequences. On the one hand, it meant that all countries and most of all industries are affected by either a single or a few number of macro economic indicator(s). At the same time, on the other hand, globalization implied that due to the existence of factor conditions(Porter 1990), within group and between group variances do exist. In other words, each country and each industry in different groups would feature divergent performance outcomes. The way this research presented this divergence is the contribution of this paper.

Second, this research, knowing the orientation of previous research tradition on economic integration, tried to provide an empirical approach by utilizing historical wage data. Analysis from this research proved to be an useful method to approach economic integration phenomenon. Thus, it would be interesting to see an updated research in the identical framework in the years to come. At the same time, it is possible to admit data limitation, which excluded several countries from analysis. A future task to develop this research, together with a revisiting one for the future, is to include diverse industrial sectors to confirm what was found in this research.

Third, in comparing the results from the 1985-1994 and 1985-2001 periods, it is possible to report an increased impact of the U.S. money supply variable in shaping the wage performance, which can be understood as industrial performance. If globalization can be understood as a phenomenon in which the impact of the most important economic variables are being increased, this research clearly supports the point. An exception to the common influence of the U.S. money factor was automobile in 1985-1994 analysis and electronics sector in 1985-2001 data. Regarding the auto sector, in 1985-2001 period, auto industry has been changed by being affected by the U.S. money variable. Electronics sector showed the opposite case. The extended period for the sector presented a divergence from the common influence of the U.S. money supply pattern. This chapter clearly presents that these changes do reflect changes in industrial landscape for the respective sector in international market places and industry structure.

## Chapter Appendix

### Table 2–3: Summary of Findings from 1985-1994 analysis

| Industrial Sector | Existence of Economic Blocs | US Money Supply as the First and Major Determinant | Importance of the US Money Supply among total wage performance(%) | Most favored group from the US Money supply changes |
|---|---|---|---|---|
| Textile | Yes | Yes | 80% | NAFTA-Asian countries |
| Automobile | Yes | No/ Second Determinant | 24.6% (second root) | Taiwan, Japan, Korea |
| Fabricated Metal | Yes | Yes | 97% | NAFTA-Asian countries |
| Industrial &Commercial machinery | Roughly Yes | Yes | 100% | EU countries |
| Shipbuilding & Repair | Yes | Yes | 80% | European countries |
| Electronics | No | Yes | 86% | European countries |

## Table 2-4 : Summary of Findings from 1990-2001 analysis

| Industrial Sector | Existence of Economic Blocs | US Money Supply as the First and Major Determinant | Importance of The US Money Supply among total wage performance(%) | Most favored group from the US Money supply changes |
|---|---|---|---|---|
| Textile | Yes | Yes | 100 % | |
| Automobile | Roughly Yes | Yes | 99.6 % | |
| Fabricated Metal | Yes | Yes | 100% | |
| Industrial &Commercial machinery | Roughly Yes | Roughly Yes | 97.7 % | |
| Shipbuilding & Repair | Yes | Yes | 100 % | |
| Electronics | No | No/Root 2 | 23% (second root) | European Group I (Fig 2-2) and Japan |
| Primary Metal | Yes | Yes | 99.9 % | |

## Table 2-5 Major Auto Manufacturing Groups

| Group | Affiliated Firms | |
|---|---|---|
| GM Group | Chevrolet, Cadillac, Pontiac, Oldsmobile, Buick, GMC, Saturn, Opel, Vaxhaul, Saab, Holden, AIOS(Turkey) Fiat Group(Fiat, Alpa Romeo, Lancia, Ferrari) Otoyol (Turkey), Isuzu, Suzuki, Maruti (India), Fuji Heavy Inc.-Subaru, Santana(Spain) GM Daewoo(Korea) | |
| Ford Group | Ford, Mercury, Lincoln, Jaguar Land-Rover, Volvo, Mazda, Aston Martin | |
| Toyota Group | Toyota, Lexus, Daihatz, Hino | |
| Daimler Chrysler Group | Chrysler, Plymouth, Dodge, Jeep Mercedes Benz, Mitsubishi | |
| Volks Wagen Group | Volks Wagen, Audi, Skoda (Checz) Rolls-Royce, Bentley Lamborogini (Italy), Scania(Sweden) | |
| Renault Group | Renault, Nissan, Mack, Infiniti Nissan Diesel, Renault-Samsung, Dachia (Romania) | |
| Other Group | Hyundai Group | Hyundai, Kia, Asia |
| | BMW Group | BMW |
| | PSA Group | Peugeot, Citroen, Talbo |
| | Honda Group | Honda, Accura |

# Chapter Appendix

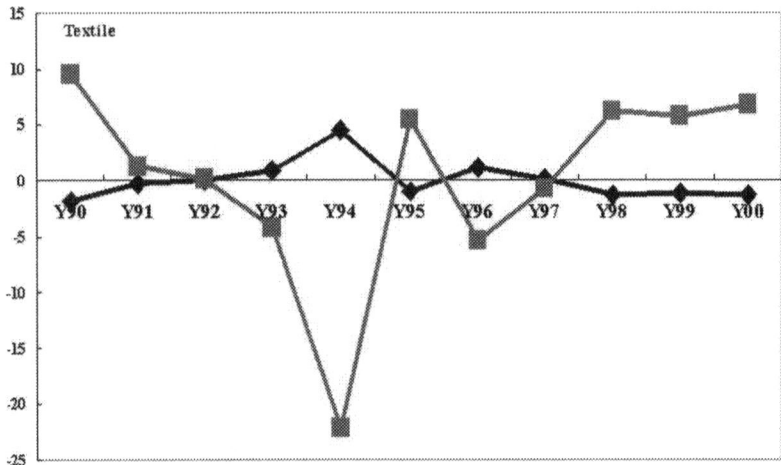

Figure 2-7 Times Series Plotting of U.S. Money and the First Root (Textile)

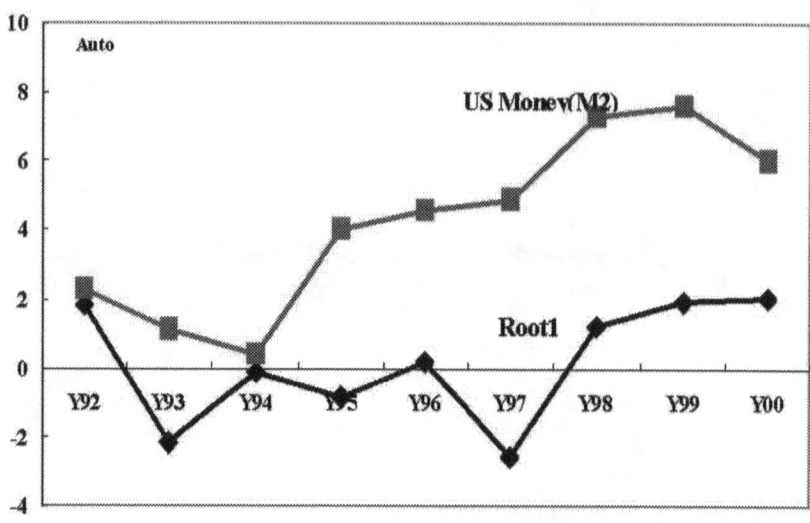

Figure 2-12 Times Series Plotting of U.S. Money and the First Root
(Auto)

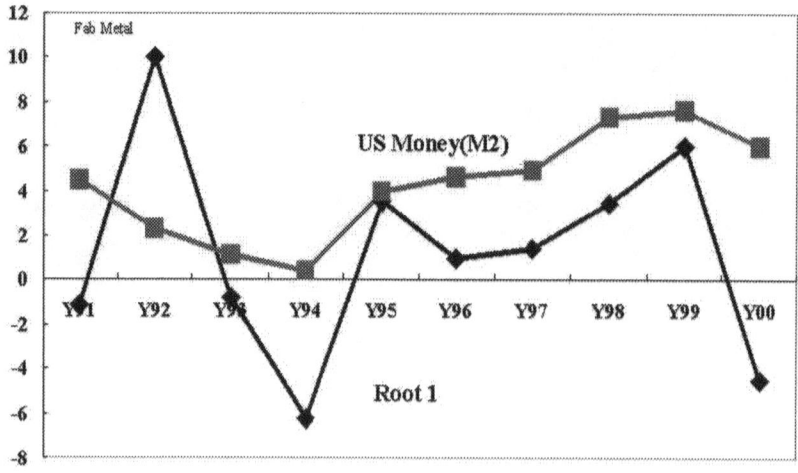

Figure 2-17 Times Series Plotting of U.S. Money and the First Root (Fab.
Metal & Machinery)

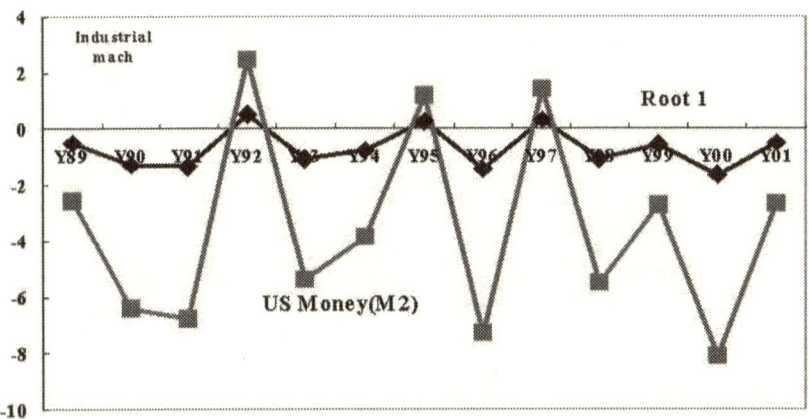

Figure 2-22 Times Series Plotting of U.S. Money and the First Root
(Industrial & Commercial Machinery)

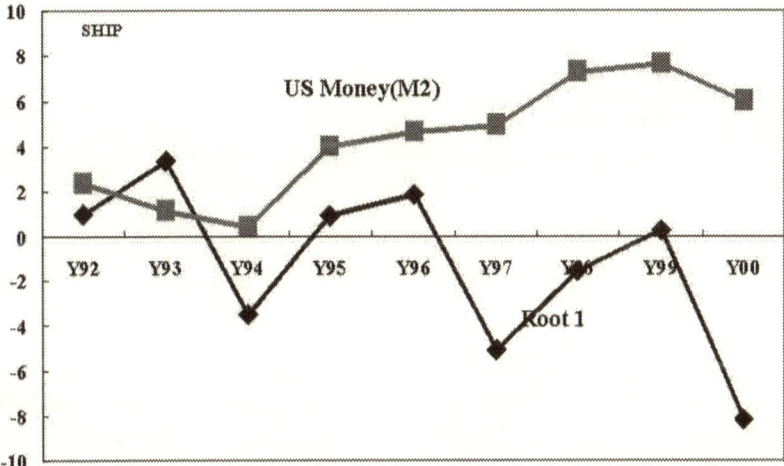

Figure 2-27 Times Series Plotting of U.S. Money and the First Root
(Ship)

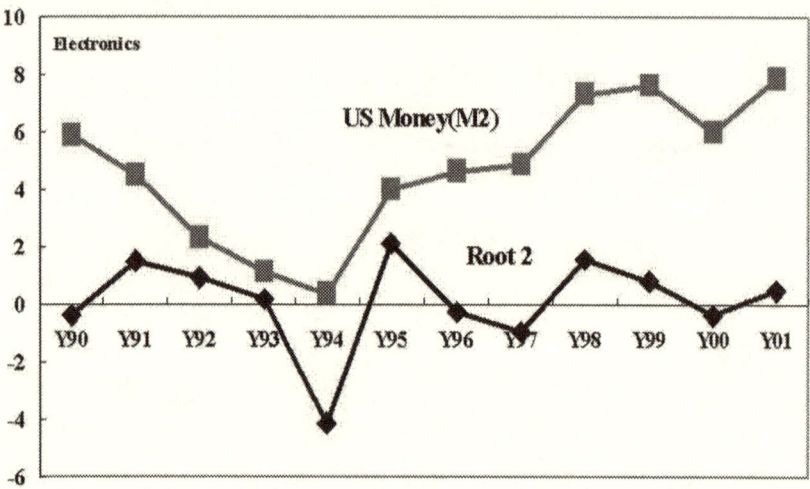

Figure 2-33 Times Series Plotting of U.S. Money and the First Root
(Electronics)

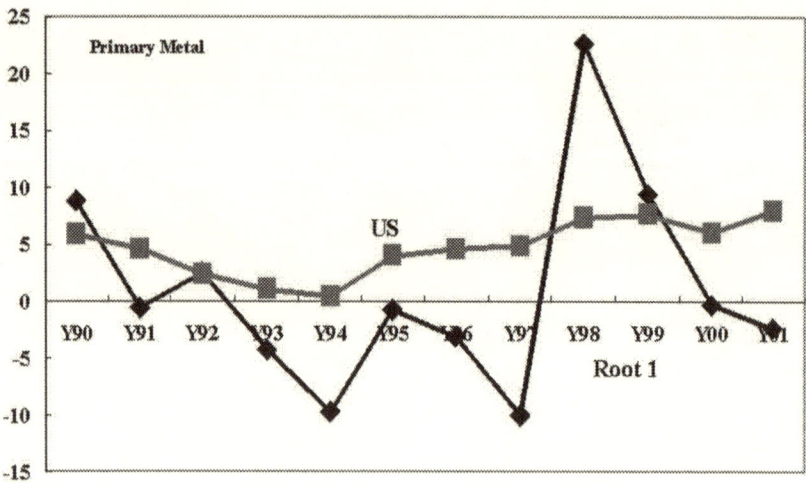

Figure 2-37 Times Series Plotting of U.S. Money and the First Root (Primary Metal)

# 3

# Dynamics of Regional Research Clusters

## Theoretical reviews on Clusters

Since the 1980s and 1990s, a great deal of attention has been given to the dynamic of clusters. The concern has been much higher and wider than its original usage in economic geography quite a long time ago. In some sense, it could be regarded as a rebirth of the concept of clusters in the new contexts. Regarding why clusters have drawn much attention, different theoretical discussions can be presented. This research, taking this as a backdrop, tried to investigate the dynamics of Regional Research Clusters with a Tri-Nation comparison of the U.S., Germany, and Korea. With a cross sectional data based regression analysis, this research has attempted to glean some interesting policy implications. First, this paper will begin with a literature review followed by the model specification, interpretation and policy implications.

### Origin of the theoretical discussion: Common roots from cluster and innovation systems

While theories on spatial distribution of industries range from traditional location theories to theories on clusters and regional innovation system, theories on clusters and regional innovation systems share some commonalities in their theoretical origin. The first commonality comes from a revision to neoclassical economics in its insufficiency to deal with technology & innovation factor. In neoclassical economics framework, either capital(K) or labor(L) is the explanatory variable, which confines technology to be melted in a combinational form of K and L. This mathematical constraint has received criticisms that the neoclassical economics has no room to accommodate organizational, institutional, technological, and cultural settings surrounding innovation.(Freeman 1987; Cooke, P. 1998a) Indeed, through the history of economics, traditional neoclassical synthesis had to 'abandon' the core contents descended from the Schumpeterian economics, which is now regarded as the 'old economic institutionalism'. Knowing the insufficiency, a group of different theoretical approaches have been proposed. These theories range from neo-Schumpeterian, neo-institutional economics, and new economic growth theories, to theories on national & regional innovation systems. Also included in the new approaches was the evolutionary economics. The gist of these new attempts has been the renewed awareness of institutions, culture and innovation as a system(Cooke, P. 1998b; Amin & Thrift 1994; Amin 1999).

The second commonality that cluster and regional innovation systems theory share has been the boom of regional studies. While there have been different forerunners, theories like flexible specialization, technopolis and discourse in economic geography has given the cluster and regional innovation system an impetus to foster their theories(Castelles & Hall 1994; Hassink 2000). In fact, the concept of cluster has been studied in economic geography in the past, which has not received attention by different groups until Michael Porter style rediscovery gave light to the concept. For Porter, the concept of cluster was a very natural extension of his theory on competitiveness, since cluster concept was imposed on his theory on competitiveness(Porter, M. 1998b).

Theories related to clusters range from research park & science park to regional innovation systems, which have been affected theoretical influences among them. While a diagram in the below can be presented as a simple map of theories, this section will focus on the discussion of clusters. In figure 1, from far left, one can find research park and science park, which are clearly artifacts to promote research performance. While there may be some arguments regarding the location of networks in this figure, network, informal and formal combined, has much wider inclusion of actors than research parks, which has compelled this section to locate next to research/science park. Cluster, in this diagram, can be regarded as a wider concept than both research/science park and network in the sense that cluster has a more natural characteristic in the way it is organized. Right to the cluster is the concept of the New Industrial District, which is typically found in Europe, including the Italian regions. In the concept of the district lies a pivotal notion of embeddedness, which clearly distinguishes the concept from others. The far right location was given to the regional innovation system, which encompasses a whole range of actors and institutions from research park, firms, public bodies, networks, and districts. The RIS, though, is a much artificial construct created to fulfill policy needs to promote effectiveness of R&D activities.

## Conceptual origin of clusters

Theories on clusters have focused on a concentration phenomenon in which geographically agglomerated production bases have developed into complementary relations among the agglomerated. Thus, a cluster is a type of a new industrial district in which hundreds of small firms are interlinked in a mutually cooperative way(Porter 1998a; 1998b; Bergman & Feser 1999; Oosterhaven et al. 2001).

The concept of cluster strongly implicates the pivotal elements of proximity and interdependence. Proximity implicates the scope of a cluster, while interdependence suggests interaction & positive feedback loop among participants of a cluster (Oosterhaven et al. 2001). To the supporters & theory developers of clusters, the world economy is nothing but a mosaic of clusters. The theory of clusters, however, has not come from vacuum. It has its own intellectual predecessors. Indeed, from the Marshallian theory of industrial location on, economic understanding of industrial location has depicted the dynamic of regional economies. Despite the lofty theoretical framework, the 20th century, especially since the post World War II era, has seen more drastic changes of economic and industrial landscape. As will be reviewed under the productivity paradox (Kim, J. 2005; Perez & Freeman 1988; Krugman 1996) section to be followed, the advanced world economies have experienced a common quandary that their investment on R&D does not seem to yield proportional benefits in terms of economic performance. In a more direct way, the more the R&D investment, it has been found that the less "visible" contribution on economic performance was possible. This has been a serious symptom, knowing the perceived impact of Science & Technology(S&T) on economic development.

One of the way to resolve the problem was to 'construct' such concepts as Technopole, technopolis and science parks. The 1980s and 1990s saw a proliferation of these concepts throughout the world, while there always have been debates on their efficacy & evaluation whether they are successful or not. While the building of technopolis & science parks have been an artificial effort per se, it is notable that direct intellectual stimuli to build such artifacts came from the case of the Silicon Valley, in which the construction & agglomeration of firms and other entities have been more natural than its successors and emulators around the world. Thus, while inheriting the intellectual and practical ancestry, the theory development of clusters has focused on a natural development of an economic dynamic in the regional settings. It is this context that the boom of cluster theory can be regarded as the rediscovery of geography, which has 'discovered' the term of clusters which had not received much attention previously.

In discussing the explanatory power and ability to describe industrial location and agglomeration, there has been a comparable concept that has been developed in Europe, namely the New Industrial District. Well integrated by Piore and Sabel (1984), the theory shows how regional & local settings can be a strong magnet of firms. A crucial selling point of the theory has been that it emphasizes not only firm side, but also shows how culture, trust, and network can be integrated to show synergy. The strong point, however, becomes its weakness in terms of theory itself. That is, the thick contents of culture-bound nature in the district are not easy to be 'emulated' in other settings, and the theory tends to be 'path-dependent', foretelling the destiny in advance. In comparison, Porter style argument can be viewed as too 'dry' by evaporating the culture bound elements. With this intellectual discourse, it is possible to infer the following.

First, in discussing regional economic dynamics, it is possible to find clusters or the New Industrial District. Second, in terms of the nature of theory, there are theories with culture-bound ones, while the other group is culture-free and more economic-side based ones. Third, no matter which side, culture bound or economic side based, a theory takes, it is possible to admit a general trend of emphasizing culture & social aspects. That is, even for the theory with economic emphasis, the importance of 'trust' is also emphasized through theories of network. Thus, it is reasonable to admit that theories by Porter also have contributed greatly in that it has offered a 'neutral' analytical framework. The next section will review Porter's theory.

## A Review of theories on industrial location
### Technopole & Technopolis, and Science Parks

Technopole or Technopolis is a concept that describes an artificial integration of research functions and its application in a geographically confined area, which has boomed since the 1970s (Castells & Hall 1994). This concept of industrial location has been called in an array of different expressions or jargons, ranging from research complex, science park, and research park to technopolis, incubation center and technopark. These different names had different starting points, but eventually have grown to mean the identical phenomenon. This can be shown by looking at the historical development. Starting from 1960s, the success of the Silicon Valley has inspired enthusiasts of the technopolis to emulate the success case. In so doing, Sophia Antipolis has been a clear example to follow the trend.

In the cases of Sophia Antipolis and Tsukuba, the emphasis has been given primarily to research, in comparison to the Silicon Valley. While Sophia Antipolis has been famous for its vast size, the British adaptation has been a much smaller variant called 'Science Park'(DTI 2001). Through the 1980s, a notable development has been the emphasis given to industrial application of research and knowledge, which naturally turned the development of industrial location to include production side into the existing research oriented sites. In Germany, this trend was exemplified as innovation centers that have been focusing on commercialization of new technologies rather than research(Cooke 1992). Despite this long change pattern, the 1990s gave a unified direction which was to add incubation and housing functions to the research complexes. As described, seemingly different concepts, in fact, have become, de facto, identical phenomenon through the adding of new functions(Kim, L.1997; Swan 1998; OECD 1999a; OECD 2001).

Since the 1970s, modeling after several forerunning exemplars, a number of countries has begun their efforts to emulate the success of earlier science parks & technopolis(Castells & Hall 1994). Despite this boom, studies have reported that about 40 to 50 % of the efforts were diagnosed as failures. (Minshall 1983, Luger 1994) Against these diagnosis, a more optimistic view exists as well. That is, the institution of technology or research complex itself takes decades of growth either continuous or divided by radical stages, which implies that a dissection-like judgment at one time would not justifiably assess the institutional success/failure of the research complex. Indeed, examples like the Sophia Antipolis, which was first started in 1968, are now being rejuvenated with new influx of firms, research centers and venture capitals.

## New Industrial District

While traditional theories of industrial location have highlighted 'pure' economic motives such as transaction costs, the main argument of the new industrial district is centered on socio-cultural aspects of location & its formation. While the root of the new industrial district comes from the Marshallian theory of industrial district, the concept of the new industrial district has been obscurely cited. Amid the confusion, it is possible to distinguish two major branches of the New Industrial District theories. One is Granovetter style theory of social relations & embeddedness that emphasize highly integrated and at the same time flexible social cohesion based on division of labor and trust. The other branch of theory comes from Michael Piore and Sabel's unique theorization(Piore & Sabel 1984). In Piore and Sabel's vision, the dynamic of New Industrial District can be summarized as follows.

First, mass production system was transplanted in Europe in the post world war II era, which resulted in a re-organization of industrial areas. Second, flexible specialization could be an alternative way of industrialization, while mass production system has been backed by political support at the world level. Third, sharing the Marshallian understanding, Piore and Sabel argues that in New Industrial District, small firms share highly skilled labor, specialized machines and even a common apprentice institutions, which are interpreted as externality effects(Capello 1999). Fourth, in New Industrial District, social cohesion among firms work as the dynamic that maintains the New Industrial District(Pisano 1989). Fifth, in flexible specialization world, it is conceivable that large & small firms can co-exist, which is not possible to be accepted in traditional economics. This feature of the flexible specialization world has been called as the dual economy.

With these characteristics, Piore & Sabel's theory has given tremendous impacts on the research of industrial districts. Their theory, however, has been faced with serious drawbacks since it was introduced. First, their theory lacks explanatory power even to embrace most of the Italian cases which vary significantly in their characteristics. For example, while the region of Tuscany featured flexibility in division of labor and cooperative social structure as its success factor, Veneto region was heavily benefited by typical low wages. Furthermore, Marche region clearly have enjoyed active involvement by local authorities as its success factor. Second, depending on authors, critics may argue that Sabel's tone has socialism in his own theory. Indeed, Piore subscribes to Boyer's regulation school argument(Boyer 2001) in his understanding of the world economy, which clearly precludes Piore & Sabel's own bias. Third, these authors have had too much confidence in the superiority of flexible specialization, while ignoring the potential of mass production system to be improved. By binding the fate of the mass production system into the fate of capitalistic growth in regulation school, flexible specialization has failed to reflect the 'real world dynamic'. Flexible specialization alone could not 'replace' the mass production world.

Despite these drawbacks, it is quite clear that scholars tended to utilize the concept of the new industrial district as a 'metaphoric way' to describe the new industrial dynamic found in the U.S., like that of Route 128 and Colorado Springs. (Markusen et al. 1991)

## Regional Innovation System

Regional Innovation System has been an adaptation from the notion of national innovation system (Lundvall 2000; Cooke et al. 1997;Cooke 1998c) in the regional settings. As the term system denotes the Regional Innovation System is a system in which all innovation actors, in a regional setting, are integrated in socio-cultural environments. The concept goes beyond a simple boundary of a technopolis or a research park in that it encompasses all arrays of institutions and even education system into the concept. Based on academic consensus, the followings can be understood as the key components of the Regional Innovation System.(Maskell & Malecki 2002)

(1) Different types of regional & local networks (Fisher, M. & Snickars 2001)

(2) Group learning & its embedded local & regional culture (Capello 1999; Fritsch, M. 2001)

(3) Trust among economic & social actors that would facilitate the infiltration of innovation into societal roots(Cooke & Morgan 1998; Hudson 1994)

(4) Institutional integrity that is fundamental to entrepreneurship(Fritsch, M. 2001)

(5) External relations that would enable the region to get over the 'lock-in' effect of path-dependency, and thereby opens new avenue & sources for innovation from outside the region

As would be understood by the key components, the trend of theory development has been made into two directions. One was a theoretical tradition that emphasizes the system concept(Lundvall 2000) and the other side can be characterized as that focuses on network itself. (Fisher, M. 1999; Gibson, David 2004; Kim, J. 2002; Keeble et al. 1999)

## Clusters

Theories on clusters have focused on a concentration phenomenon in which geographically agglomerated production bases have developed into complementary relations among the agglomerated. Thus, a cluster is a type of a new industrial district in which hundreds of small firms are interlinked in a mutually cooperative way(Porter 1998a; 1998b; Bergman & Feser 1999; Oosterhaven et al. 2001).

Developed originally from the discipline of geography, cluster theory has received glamorous footlights with the introduction by Michael Porter, who has applied the cluster concept to his notion of Diamond type competitiveness theory(Lagendijk 1997; Yamawaki 2002). Reflecting the origin of cluster that comes from the lineage of theory development(Lorenz & Lawson 1999; Saxenian 1994; Rantisi 2002) from the new industrial district, to networks and RIS, Porter defined a cluster as a network of suppliers, final consumers, user firms, and producers that are linked to production chains, yet maintain independence.

Despite public attention to the concept of clusters by Porter, his theory has been criticized for the following grounds. First, his theory has treated external factors of firms in a simplistic way. Second, his theory has too much emphasis on the application side of knowledge, and not the production & diffusion sides of knowledge, which is a clear demarcation between Porter's and other theorists on industrial location & innovation(Giaccaria 1999). Third, his theory has neglected spatial side of an innovation location. Fourth, since his theory emphasized geographical proximity and competitiveness(Timothy 2001), Porter's theory is sharply contrasted with other theories that emphasize cooperation. Fifth, critics have implied that while Porter has applied different theories in the development of his argument on clusters, his theory has not showed a clear understanding on the essence of embeddedness and network, which are crucial to clusters.

Succeeding the popularity and attention on clusters, public discussion on clusters found an exit by converting the concept of clusters into innovation clusters by including the actors of innovation, which are universities, public research institutions, consulting firms, and other knowledge intensive business firms. (OECD 1999b) This can be understood as a definite synthesis of theories aimed at practical application.

## Michael Porter's theory on Clusters

### Porter's Theory on Competitiveness: an adaptation to regional settings

Developed originally from the discipline of geography, cluster theory has received glamorous footlights with the introduction by Michael Porter, who has applied the cluster concept to his notion of Diamond type competitiveness theory(Lagendijk 1997; Yamawaki 2002). Reflecting the origin of cluster that comes from the lineage of theory development(Lorenz & Lawson 1999; Saxenian 1994; Rantisi 2002) from the new industrial district, to networks and RIS, Porter defined a cluster as a network of suppliers, final consumers, user firms, and producers that are linked to production chains, yet maintain independence.

For Porter, an application of his competitiveness model to a regional setting is clearly revealed. Porter argues that the success of a region depends on i) vertical relations of sales & purchases and ii) a horizontal relations of technology, cooperation, and communication. In utilizing the characteristics in his model, Porter presents his diamond model, which consists of the four factors of competition, demand, factor conditions, and related support industries, which were originally presented in his explanation of national competitiveness. In his model, Porter argues that through "incentives for change", competitive environments can be created, through which pre-existing inertia can be overcome. This is equivalent to divert from the notion of "path-dependency", which has been generally thought to exist and not perish.

Once cluster is formed, it has several claimed advantages. First, cluster reduces costs to produce, diffuse, and apply knowledge & information, and thereby improve economic performance in the regional economy. Second, cluster helps firms to actualize not only economies of scale, but also economies of scope. Third, by utilizing clusters, risks & costs of R&D can be shared among participants.

### Critiques on porter's theory on clusters

Despite public attention to the concept of clusters by Porter, his theory has been criticized for the following grounds. First, his theory has treated external factors of firms in a simplistic way. Second, his theory has too much emphasis on the application side of knowledge, and not the production & diffusion sides of knowledge, which is a clear demarcation between Porter's and other theorists on industrial location & innovation(Giaccaria 1999). Third, his theory has neglected spatial side of an innovation location. Fourth, since his theory emphasized geographical proximity and competitiveness(Timothy 2001), Porter's theory is sharply contrasted with other theories that emphasize cooperation. Fifth, critics have implied that while Porter has applied different theories in the development of his argument on clusters, his theory has not showed a clear understanding on the essence of embeddedness and network, which are crucial to clusters.

## Innovation Clusters

The notion of innovation clusters encompasses the scope of discussion from Porter's clusters and Regional Innovation Systems(RIS). The basic notion of RIS can be summarized as follows.

Regional Innovation System has been an adaptation from the notion of national innovation system (Lundvall 2000; Cooke et al. 1997;Cooke 1998c) in the regional settings. As the term system denotes the Regional Innovation System is a system in which all innovation actors, in a regional setting, are integrated in socio-cultural environments. The concept goes beyond a simple boundary of a technopolis or a research park in that it encompasses all arrays of institutions and even education system into the concept.

The trend of theory development regarding the R.I.S. has been made into two directions. One was a theoretical tradition that emphasizes the system concept(Lundvall 2000) and the other side can be characterized as that focuses on network itself. (Fisher, M. 1999; Gibson, David 2004; Kim, J. 2002; Keeble et al. 1999)

The grand scheme of the theory of Regional Innovation System allows the theory to have a greater explanatory power. This advantage, however, has a crucial disadvantage found in other theories with 'all powerful' explanatory power, like historical institutionalism found in social science tradition. By encompassing every element that has to do with explanation, the theory of Regional Innovation System has resulted in explaining nothing. In comparison, another branch of Regional Innovation System theory variant, network theories have focused on micro dynamic of networks in innovation systems.

In comparison, theoretical discussion on clusters found an exit by converting the concept of clusters into innovation clusters by including the actors of innovation, which are universities, public research institutions, consulting firms, and other knowledge intensive business firms. (OECD 1999b) This can be understood as a definite synthesis of theories aimed at practical application.

## Productivity Paradox

Advanced economies have experienced a common phenomenon called the productivity paradox (Kim, J. 2005; Perez & Freeman 1988; Krugman 1996) since the 1970s on, which shows that the increase of R&D expenditure has not been matched with the increased contribution from the research on economic performance. This has been attributed to the increase of complexity from R&D via the application of research findings to actual economic performance (Kim, J. 2005). In fact, diverse government efforts to promote research functions including science parks, research clusters and regional innovation systems can all be regarded as concerted efforts to overcome the phenomenon. In designing research models, this paper has tried to reflect this aspect, as long as data permits the analysis.

## Results from Regression Models
## Data

With the theories reviewed, to design a well functioning R&D network at national level, it is crucial to identify critical success factors. To empirically approach the factors, this research attempted a tri-nation comparative research, which utilized the U.S. German, and Korean data sets for cross sectional OLS regression analysis. For the U.S data, this study used the U.S. Government's Office of Technology Policy(OPM)'s State Science and Technology Indicators from *The Dynamics of Technology based Economic Development*. As for the German data, this paper adopted the Report of the Federal Government on Research(2000) published by the German government. For the Korean data, Ministry of Science & Technology(MOST) data was utilized. With the data, this paper reports results from a regression analysis.

## Common Policy issues from the Critical Factors

Through the analysis, this research has attempted to analyze the dynamic of national & regional networks, with respect to the critical factors of R&D budget, man power policy, and specific national issues (Luger 1994), in the U.S., Germany, and Korea. In designing & implementing regression models, this research has focused on specific policy issues relevant in each country's contexts, while trying to maintain comparability in the countries. In fact, differences in data structure, an exactly identical model building was not possible. Despite these commonalities and differences, several common policy issues can be presented before presenting specific national issues that have international attention.

## Public R&D

In both the U.S. and Korean cases, one of the critical concerns from a public policy point of view has been regarding the impact of public R&D. In the U.S. case, all specifications showed that the public R&D was a statistically meaningful variable, which had stronger impact than the private R&D. Public R&D in the U.S. had a positive impact on the dependent variable. A striking finding was that the gross R&D had a negative impact on the dependent variable, the state GDP. This can be interpreted as complexity of linkage from research to wealth creation in the U.S. has made the impact of the gross R&D smaller and eventually turned into negative side. Also this should be understood in the global context that other advanced countries have experienced the identical case (Kim, J 2005a).

In both German and Korean case, the public(federal) R&D variable consistently showed negative contribution on the provincial GDP, the dependent variable, which can be understood in the same vein as the U.S. gross R&D variable case. Regarding the interpretation on the public R&D, the following points can be raised.

First, it is, in general, plausible to accept as a global phenomenon that complexity of linkage from research to wealth creation has been increased, which will increase potentials to have negative impacts of research funds on economic performance. Second, among the three countries, it is reasonable to infer that university based research funds in Germany and the U.S. public R&D funds have been used in a more market friendly way, judging from the contribution of the variable on economic performance. This reflects a tendency of research tradition in the two countries. In the U.S., gross level R&D expenditures at the societal level showed a negative impact on economic performance, which can be explained as the productivity paradox in R&D (Kim, J 2005a).

## Man Power Strategy

In the U.S. case, the education level variables revealed that the number of Ph.D. holders had the greatest impact on GDP, followed by the number of Bachelor's degree holders and the number of master's degree holders. The finding that the number of Bachelor's degree holders had greater impact than the number of master's degree holders implies a unique R&D manpower structure of the U.S. economy, which signifies that the economy's R&D system is led by Ph.D. level researchers plus production level Bachelor's degree holders. In the German and Korean data, an exactly identical specification was not possible. In the German case, the number of university based researchers, as a variable, was a variable that had consistently negative impact on the Land GDP. This was a clear contrast to the finding that in German case, university based funds had the strongest impact on the wealth creation at Land level. In the Korean case, instead, a comparison, between the number of researchers at universities and the number of researchers at firms, was performed. It showed almost similar impact on the provincial GDP.

## Specific National issues

### The role of Ph.D. level researchers in the U.S. context

As mentioned, the degree of relative contribution of Ph.D. level researchers on economic performance was found to be greater than the Master's or Bachelor's degree level researchers. This clearly has a policy implication in designing educational system for the engineering & natural science fields. Assuming that capacity of education system in a country is given at a time frame, it would be wise to have a system that can maximize the potential contribution to the economy. In this vein, an emphasis to foster Ph.D. degrees in engineering and science fields will be crucially important. Due to data limitations, the identical specifications were not possible, but it is quite reasonable to infer that similar situations have been in place in many advanced economies since the 1960s on, namely the shortage of research man power. A policy option to resolve and improve this finding would be to enhance the current educational grants and scholarships to induce more talented students to choose the engineering track. A more important incentive mechanism, however, is to let the graduates of engineering degrees to stay in their majoring fields after graduation. Statistics from the advanced economies have evidenced that engineering fields degree holders had flexibility to move to business (like M.B.A) or medical fields following higher labor rents, expressed in wages. This has been inter-preted as their capability in mathematical education has easily enabled them to move to other areas.

## The Former East German Lands in the German case

To both for outside observers as well as policy makers inside, the consequences from the unification is of great interest. Analysis from this research shows at least a partial dissection of the dynamics of research clusters in Germany, which can be summarized in two points. One is that in terms of absolute size of research related funds and budget, the former west is far superior in every indicator. In contrast, for the former East German lands, it is a common find-ing that each land was trying its best to channel resources for the R&D activi-ties. The other point is that in terms of efficiency of R&D expenditure, some of the most affluent lands in the former West German areas marked lower grades. This gives us two interpretations: One would be that in the western lands, public R&D has been utilized in a "real" public and long term purposed basic research, while the former eastern areas had to concentrate on a more direct link from research to actual economic performance. The other interpre-tation would be that the western lands clearly show the symptoms of produc-tivity paradox (Kim, J. 2005; Perez & Freeman 1988; Krugman 1996) shared by other advanced economies.

## Center/Periphery argument in the Korean case

As reported in the preceding section, this research tried to analyze the *Center/ Periphery* argument. Based on the findings from this research, the *Center/ Periphery* difference was not a strong variable to withstand different specifica-tions. Thus, it is too early to preclude that the variable had a meaningful impact, since some provinces showed that their potentials to increase provin-cial GDP with other policy variables in the model.

With the analysis, it was possible to present common policy issues shared by the three countries, while, at the same time, specific national contexts could be discussed. In analyzing, it was understood that limitations from the differ-ences of data structure have precluded the exact comparison of the three coun-tries. Also, in need was the necessity to have a time series analysis with similar specifications, which can be forwarded for a future study.

# Case Studies of France & Sweden

## *Kista cluster of Sweden*

Kista Science City is located at 15 minutes distance from Arlanda airport and 15 minutes from Stockholm City. In many respects, the region extends across four municipalities around Järvafältet. It also has the advantage of proximity to Sweden's financial centres in Stockholm, and the strong biomedical developments in the area from Uppsala, across the Karolinska Institutet medical university in Huddinge/Södertälje

Globally recognized as the Wireless and Mobile Valley, Kista is the heart of Sweden's IT industry with more than 375 high-tech companies, ranging from university spin-offs to world-leading corporations. Companies such as Ericsson, IBM, Nokia, TietoEnatro, Oracle, Aligent, Intel, HP, Apple and ADC already have offices, and Nokia, TietoEnator, HP, Microsoft, Sun Microsystems, Intel, and Huawci, ZTE and Oracle have research facilities., while the largest company in Kista is Ericsson, with approximately 8,000 employees in 2003. The company invested a total of SEK 40 billion in research and development in 2001 and the head office for the company's research division is located in Kista. Ericsson has transferred its group head office to Kista in 2003 in order to be closer to its operations.

In the core areas of Kista district, some 27,000 people work in over 700 companies in 2003. Two-thirds of them are employed by companies working in the ICT area. In the greater Kista Science City area some 65,000 people work. Kista holds its own as a leading IT cluster. In 2002, the German consulting firm Empirica Delasasse gave a ranking to 214 European regions, in which Stockholm and Kista were placed in the top tier. Kista Science City received a special mention as being a successful case of close collaboration between academia and the business community. Kista is home to numerous research-intensive companies. Many examples of innovative, entrepreneurial start-ups can be found here, such as Neonode, Printdreams and Senseboard. IT and telecommunications are the common denominators for most of the innovation companies in the area, which are Mobile services, wireless systems and broadband systems. In 2003, the Italian business analysis firm Fondazione Rosselli extended this study to include the USA. The study showed Sweden as having the world's best climate for innovation. In the areas of technology and scientific expertise, human capital and financial resources for research and development, Sweden clearly shows competitiveness with similar examples like Finland. In table below, it is possible to infer a time series trend of ICT concentration in Kista region. As shown, the proportion of ICT sector has increased from 43% in 1986 to an average of 60 plus % through the 1990s and 2000s. Despite the fact that the statistical category does not reflect, among the numbers in the non-ICT sectors exist advanced service sector which are also a symbol of regional economic competitiveness.

**Table 3-1 Total employment by types of firms in Kista District 1990-2004 [*]**

|  | 1990 | 1994 | 1996 | 1998 | 2000 | 2001 | 2002 | 2003 |
|---|---|---|---|---|---|---|---|---|
| ICT Firms (A) | 12699 | 10737 | 15023 | 17307 | 18065 | 19023 | 18354 | 18114 |
| Non-ICT Firms (B) | 9136 | 7564 | 9590 | 9288 | 9615 | 9417 | 8209 | 9213 |
| Total #of Employees(C) | 19873 | 20263 | 24613 | 26595 | 27680 | 28440 | 26563 | 27327 |
| (A)/(C) | 0.639008 | 0.529882 | 0.610369 | 0.650761 | 0.652637 | 0.668882 | 0.690961 | 0.662861 |

[*]　2004 statistics are based on the first half of the year.

## Related Institutions in KISTA
## IT University

In Kista area, it is possible to mention the existence of key institutions that make the Kista a working cluster. IT is a broad area of research and the link between the University of Stockholm and KTH (The Royal Institute of Technology) has become apparent when research from the IT University is presented. The University of Stockholm contributes with the social aspects and KTH with the technical. Campus Kista also has five research centres with different specialty areas. Most of them are widely recognized internationally and have close connections with the business community. Kista Photonics Research Center is the latest entity to join.

## Research institutes

Kista is home to three research institutes with different areas of focus and activities: Acreo, Sics and STFI/Packforsk.

### Swedish Institute of Computer Science (SICs)

Swedish Institute of Computer Science (SIC) is a widely recognized research institute at which almost 100 research scientists work within the fields of computer and systems science. Fascinating research projects conducted at the seven laboratories cover all areas from human-machine interaction to tomorrow's Internet technology. Industry and academia can be found working closely alongside these research projects. Sics also has a well-developed international network.

### Acreo: Microelectronics and optics

With its core activities in Kista, Norrköping and Hudiksvall Acreo is one of Sweden's largest research institutes in the field of microelectronics and optics. Work is conducted in close collaboration with industry and the institute is also highly successful when it comes to spin-offs and innovations.

### STFI/Packforsk

On the first of January 2003, the two research institutes STFI and Packforsk were integrated. The idea was to become an international centre for research and development in the fields of pulp, paper and packaging materials and logistics. The new institute serves two major industrial clusters—the forest industry and the packaging industry.

### Sophia Anti polis of France
### Project Initiation

Sophia Antipolis was first planned by Pierre Lafitte, a renowned scholar as a futuristic research city in 1968. As for France, aster passing through the world war II reconstruction era, a necessity to reduce the gap between the great Paris and other areas has been felt in regional development policy point of view. Located at a 20 minute distance from the Nice International airport and TGV high speed train station, and adjacent to the shore of Côte d'Azur, Sophia Antipolis has been endowed with all the "blessings" that research/science city should be equipped with.

In terms of major landmarks of development,

- In 1969, Sophia Antipolis association was established

- In 1972, a land use plan was announced, in which a third of total space is allocated to research facilities & housing, while the remaining two-thirds are maintained as "green belt". Since 1972 on, 2,300 hectare are size land has been developed, while another 1,600 hectare are development is in process with delays due to objections from NGOs.

## Local body of Development

After the initiation of Pierre Lafitte, Sophia Antipolis association with assistance from the central government, a local institution, Symisa, was created to work in the purchases & sales of land in Sophia Antipolis region. This institution was made of city officials, local chamber of commerce members and participants from other related institutions. In 1990s, agglomeration of cities became legally available for small municipalities around the Sophia Antipolis, which prompted them to form CASA, which is an institution for regional administration among local entities. Between CASA and Symisa, there has been a tension regarding policies & politics on Sophia Antipolis.

## The Role of Central Government

Although the role of local governments have been important in the development of Sophia Antipolis, the role of central government has been also critical. Délégation à l'aménagement du territoire et à l'action régionale (DATAR), established in 1963, has been the central government's arm in regional development, which influenced firms to move into Sophia Antipolis area through the 1970s. In fact, 1970s saw the location decision by Air France reservation & computing center and other large companies in the Sophia Antipolis area. What is noteworthy is that France had its own vision of networking. In the 1970s with the use of IT technology, long before the commercial use of Internet, the French initiative was something called the "minitel", a text service based networking system that enabled value added information services. With IT technology based on minitel, the French idea was that it was possible to locate computing centers afar from Paris in Sophia Antipolis. DATAR has shown reduced influence in 1980s, but government research labs, CNRS, continued to move into the Sophia Antipolis area through the 1980s.

## Major Achievements by Period

* The First Growth period (1970s through the early 1990s)

The first growth period can be characterized as exogenous growth in the sense that large corporations from outside entered the Sophia Antipolis region, which caused the growth of Sophia Antipolis. Large corporations, in this context, include both MNCs and large French firms. Major examples include the reservation center of Air France that has been induced by fine information infra structure. Due to exogenous nature of entrant firms and organizations, it was not feasible to find and hire locally raised research manpower, which resulted in bringing in the research manpower from outside. This has caused a serious consequences of detaching indigenous and exogenous factors of innovation systems, in which exogenous factors denote firms from outside. Also, the first growth period has ended with the MNCs began migrating to more labor cost wise competitive areas in the former Eastern Europe.

Figure 3-1 Adjacent Municipalities around the Sophia Antipolis

* The Second Growth period (1990s on)

After a downturn from 1992 to 1994, the Sophia Antipolis region has met the Second Growth period. A major & critical difference of the period vis-à-vis the first period was the endogenous growth factor of this period. In other words, venture capital firms and other locally developed firms became growth engine of the region. On this, there is an insightful argument from the downturn of the first growth period. When the MNC based research labs began migrating from the Sophia Anti polis to other European sites, it seemed inevitable that locally recruited personnels lost their jobs. The research manpower became the backbone of the growth engine in the second growth period. This period also noted the development of local indigenous research networks like the T.V.(Telecomm valley) in which U.S. firms like the Texas Instrument, French Telecom, local SMEs and French government funded CNRS participated.

## An Assessment on the Sophia Antipolis

Regarding assessment of Sophia Antipolis, it has been possible to raise several criticisms, which have reduced their validity in the later stages of development. First, policies on Sophia Antipolis development has been criticized for accumulating firms, labs and other entities in an atmosphere in which no cooperation was made. Second, in general, Sophia Antipolis region has experienced a non-network situation among researcher groups, which would otherwise created synergy of the region. Third, between firms and labs that came from outside and CNRS, there has been distance in relationships. Fourth, there has been an argument that Sophia Antipolis area has been less successful in creating strong local SMEs.

In sum, all these four factors are intertwined that is it possible to start explaining with one element. In Sophia Antipolis area labor & wages and general management costs level have been relatively high, while infra structure related services has not been sufficient. Together with these, working conditions at large firms have been far superior enough to discourage researchers and workers at large firms and labs to make spin-offs from their existing workplaces. All three factors strengthened the locational factor for large firms that would internalize R&D. A consequence has been relatively less developed SMEs. This explains other three criticisms on Sophia Antipolis in the previous paragraphs as well, which altogether have been ameliorated.

Despite the criticisms, as this chapter has described, the adjustment period of 1992 to 1994 created a new momentum from which the existing inertias were broken. The cut-off research manpower became the critical resources for local start-ups, which makes the existing criticism on Sophia Antipolis an "old story" In this sense, Sophia Antipolis as an example of regional development and science & research city can be regarded as a case of natural maturation & success. As of 2001 & 2002 period, statistics shows that the area of Sophia Antipolis holds the following entities and key man power: 1.259 companies, 25.911 jobs, 148 foreign capital companies, 68 nationalities among the staff and 4.000 researchers and 4500 students.

# 4

# Dynamics of Innovation Network Building between Research Institutions and Small & Medium Enterprises(SME)s

As the 21st century opens up, salience of technology development gathers greater attention inheriting full thrust from the 1990s. In designing a strategy for science & technology development, with its intellectual tradition mainly from the 1980s, one of the clear trends has been the network building.(Debresson & Amesse 1991; Levy & Samuelson 1991; Drucker 1998) Confronted with similar external & internal changes, advanced countries in the Western Hemisphere have pursued a policy trend of "network" building, materialized as science & technology networks and the National Innovation System (Nelson 1993; OECD 1997a; Lundvall 1992; Sandholtz 1992; EC 1995). Rationale behind the network comes from a phenomenon called 'productivity paradox (Kim, J. 2005) that these countries have commonly experienced through the 1970s (Perez & Freeman 1988; Krugman 1996). The phenomenon, being that benefits from science & technology investment increase at an unproportionally lower rates with an unit increase of science & technology investment, has become a serious social issue as the economies became more reliant on the development of science & technology (Nelson & Romer 1996; Rosenberg 1996, 1982; Conceição, Heitor and Oliveira 1998; Dosi 1988). Networking was proposed as a way to cope with the problem.

While the above mentioned dynamic has been the major trend in the advanced nations, developing countries, such as Korea, although it has waded through a different development track, seem to share the necessity of science & technology policy network building as a way to cope with new environments. With this context, this paper focuses on the feasibility of research network building between government-funded research institutions and Small & Medium enterprises (SMEs) by surveying researchers at both sides. The aim of the survey can be articulated in two ways. First, by asking highly experienced researchers at government labs who already accumulated cooperative research experience with SMEs in Korea on the feasibility of research network building in a more formal way than they had experienced, this research tried to deduce policy implications of research network building in Korea with eventual aim of providing a generalizable argument. Second, since this paper utilized existing theories on research networks, the utilization endowed this research with an opportunity to test theoretical arguments in the Korean contexts for policy implications.

## Salience of Network
### Informal Network

The importance of network in science & technology community comes from a fact that the possibility that a scientific and technological achievement can be attained by one individual is being reduced in great degrees with increasing nature of science & technology field as a system integration field. In this regard, it is possible to infer inevitable reliance on networks from the characteristics of knowledge. Typically, people distinguish explicit and implicit or tacit knowledge. The critical importance of network in science & technology field comes from the nature of implicit knowledge. Against generalists' view on science & technology field, it is not feasible to 'record' all necessary ideas and know-hows in codes, including mathematics. In this regard, for high-end and the most advanced knowledge in each field is likely to be in existence in a form of non-codified state, which means that only people who are 'embodied' with that knowledge can explain and apply that knowledge.

It is this context that informal network gets its meaning. In some sense, the beginning of informal network or networking starts when people exchange their business cards at such meetings as academic conferences, seminars, colloquium, and other relevant meetings. In a typical joke in professional world is that it is possible to locate some one who you know only by names by asking less than 10 people. This basic idea, in some sense, can be applied across national borders in each specialized field. Thus, the most standard and well known channels of informal networks are academic community and universities, where actors from diverse circles can exchange their ideas even with hiding their most intrinsic motives, though there are always possibilities their seemingly hidden agendas can be deciphered by others.

The most important element in understanding informal networks, however, comes from their informal nature. That is, despite the point that there exist formal networks, the pivotal element or sufficient condition to have any kind networks is the nature of informal networks. If there is a formal network with less content of informal networks inside, it would be a 'dry' network in which only contract based relationships prevail. Furthermore, a formal network, with no or minimal informal bondage, would imply that the formal network is fragile enough to be disbanded. Examples of industry consortia in different countries can be examples. Among informal networks, informal networks made by engineers in practitioners' circle can be distinguished with the previous description of informal network in two ways. One is that the way participants interact would be more selective than the general informal networks. Second, the degrees of tacit knowledge exchanged are increased, and participants would try to co-operative only when mutual interests can be guaranteed (Hipple 1987). In this community, individual reputation gets important.

## Formal Network

In contrast to informal network, formal network has binding relationships including contracts. Despite this difference, the motive to initiate formal networks comes from applied field informal networks composed of practitioners. Due to their strong motives for co-operation, feasibilities to launch formal networks are increased.

## Clusters and networks

For clusters, it would be possible to distinguish between cluster in the sense of geographical concentration and innovation clusters. This chapter can take both cases in the discussion of the relationship between clusters and networks. It is possible to think of a case in which there is little informal or formal network even in a cluster area. In comparison, the concept of network enables the network be formed between and among entities outside a single cluster zone.

In this sense, clusters themselves do no guarantee the existence and development of networks, while networks themselves can be regarded as sufficient condition to have a successful cluster, if a successful cluster can be understood as that with both geographical proximity and informal networking.

## R&D and Network: Stages of Innovation

From a point of R&D, it is possible to present at least two typologies in which the importance of network gets stronger meanings.

**Table 4–1 R&D Model I: Generational Typology I**

| R&D generations | Context | Key Characteristic |
|---|---|---|
| 1st Generation | Black Hole Demand Model -from 1950s to mid 1960s | R&D as Ivory Tower |
| 2nd Generation | Market share model -from mid 1960s to early 1970s | R&D as business |
| 3rd Generation | Rationalization model -from mid 1970s to mid 1980s | R&D as Portfolio |
| 4th Generation | Limited Time model -from early 1980s to mid 1990s | R&D as Integrative activity |
| 5th Generation | System Integration Model -from mid 1990s to present | R&D as Network |

Adapted & Developed from the following literature

(**Nobelius 2004;**Chiesa 2001; Miller & Morris 1998)

The 1$^{st}$ generation of R&D has been regarded as the Ivory tower style activity. In this R&D activity, all other organizational departments, except the R&D related ones, are not linked through interactions with the R&D department. R&D, in this case, is seen as a kind of Overhead costs to be spent, and that is why R&D is expressed in the Black Hole Demand Model. The second generation model is called the Market share model, since R&D is regarded as a tool to be engaged in the market share battle of a firm. In this conceptualization, R&D activities are understood to be located under the umbrella of project management. As the notion of R&D gets into the third generation, the idea evolves through the concept of portfolio. Now R&D is regarded as something to do with corporate strategic perspective. The fourth generation model would emphasize the integrative activities of R&D, which implies that R&D is now making distance with the product focus, while reducing the gap between the R&D and customers. The fifth generation understands R&D as network. Now R&D is understood to be "located" in the midst of suppliers, distributors, competitors and other relevantly recognized actors that would form the network of R&D. In this notion, it is argued that the ability to control product development speed gets importance, and thereby Research and Development may be separated.

### Tabel 4-2 R&D Model II: Generational Typology II

|  | 1$^{st}$ Generation | 2$^{nd}$ Generation | 3$^{rd}$ Generation | 4$^{th}$ Generation |
|---|---|---|---|---|
| AssetIn R&D | Technology | Project | Enterprise | Customers/Clients |
| Overview of R&D(One word image) | R&D as an Isolated Island | R&D as Linkage with Business | R&D as Integration of technology and business | R&D as Integration of technology with Customers/Clients |

## Tabel 4-2 R&D Model II: Generational Typology II (Continued)

| Motives for R&D& Consequences | R&D regarded asOverhead costs | R&D regarded asCost sharing | R&D regarded asa balance between risks & compensation | R&D regarded asa way to ameliorate Productivity Paradox |
|---|---|---|---|---|
| Organizational structure | Hierarchy | Matrix type | Distributed Co-ordination | Multi-Dimensional Multi tasking |
| Manpower strategy | Competition among groups | Pre-coordinated cooperation | Organized cooperation | Concentration on capability & value |
| Process Management | Minimal communication | Individual project as a unit | Purpose oriented R&D | Feed backs |

As shown the table 4-2, in the first generation model, technology itself was pursued as an isolated island model. In this pursuit, R&D was regarded as Overhead costs, which is an inevitable cost component. In the first model, the R&D organization was a hierarchical one with minimal communication and competition among groups has been the norms. As the model changes into the 2nd generation, R&D is a 'project', in which cost sharing is pursued. In this model, as for the organizational form, matrix type organization is preferred. A noteworthy point is that in the second model, individual project is regarded as a unit. In the third generational model, now R&D is viewed from a bigger picture, enterprise. In this perspective, R&D is understood as an integration of technology and business, in which a balance between risks & compensation is sought. For organizational structure, a distributed coordination model is utilized. In the fourth generational model in table 4-2, R&D is regarded as an integration of technology with Customers/Clients. The motive to engage into R&D activities is to ameliorate Productivity Paradox phenomenon (Kim, J. 2005). As for the way R&D organization is managed, a multi tasking structure is utilized. In understanding the different generational models, it would be fair to think that latter models would naturally inherit previous notions in previous models. For example, in asset, the point that clients are emphasized in the 4th generational model does not necessarily mean that the model does not appreciate technology as asset. Rather it would be reasonable to understand the previous virtues of assets will naturally be inherited to the coming models. Also noteworthy is that the models will only be an abstracted ideal type paradigm, which means that, in real world, a more diverse combination of R&D models would possibly be in existence.

Clear from the two typologies, however, for the discussion of this chapter on network is that as time passes by the nature of R&D is getting closer to what network theory has been foretelling, which clearly reflects the nature of science & technology fields that have increased the complexities through recent decades. The evidence of network components can easily be found in both typologies. With table 4-2, from the notion of asset to organizational structure and manpower strategy, everything component explicitly and implicitly signals that there is network component in the models as they develop into the later models.

## Global context of Network Building

In understanding the salience of research networks, it is reasonable to track several key developments that have been shared among advanced economies since the Post-war economic boom, which are closely inter-connected to deduce the research network. These key developments include the relative decline of Fordism(Berger 1982), Productivity paradox (Kim, J. 2005), and the gradual reduction of enrollment in engineering schools.

Fordism or Mass-Production system that has been the pillar of economic growth since the Post-war period had its system requirements including a stable macro economic management by government, namely the Keynesian Demand Management policy, which became more difficult to maintain.(Boyer 1988; Boltho 1982) While several factors have contributed to the relative decline, from a technology perspective, the decline implied that production system of the future would require either an input of more intensive use of technology or a paradigm change into "flexible specialization"(Piore & Sable 1984; Shimada 1991). The course taken was adopting both. Flexible specialization inspired mass production system to be flexible as exemplified by such system as Just-In-Time(JIT). More importantly, however, the other path, intensive use of technology naturally called the importance science &

technology as the main engine for growth (Nelson & Romer 1996; Freeman 1987; Rosenberg 1996,1982; Dosi 1988; Sandholtz 1992). This emphasis brought a dilemma, since from the 1970s on advanced economies began experiencing a phenomenon called "productivity paradox" (Perez & Freeman 1988; Krugman 1996; Kim, J. 2005).

Furthermore, an important pillar of science & technology promotion, the supply of science & engineering students has decreased in advanced economies, which indirectly evidences that pays in science & technology research positions have been lower than their private sector equivalents or substitutes (Pearson 1990; OECD 1989).

(Institutionalization)

With these developments, trend for research network building was accelerated.[1](Metcalfe 1990; NBIA 1998; Oh & Masser 1995; Porter 1998; Rullani 1988) Behind the development lies an important under-current of increasing complexity of science & technology and its application, i.e. system integration characteristic, in which one researcher's effort is less likely to make a decisive contribution.

In Europe, the concept of National Innovation System (NIS) in which various levels of research units are interconnected has emerged.(Freeman 1987;OECD 1997; Lundvall 1992; Nelson 1993) Similar in vein and as a part of National Innovation System, science park or research oriented cities were constructed with linkages being built around regional research units such as universities, firms, and business incubators. (Masser 1989, 1991; Grayson 1993; Kawamoto 1992; Koschatzky & Kulicke 1994; Luger 1994; Sung 1997; Tatsuno 1986; Segal 1985; Monck et al. 1985)

## The Korean Context

While Asian countries like Korea have been known as a serious practitioner of industrial policy (Kim, J 1999,2000;Galbraith & Kim 1998), with increasing globalization and its accompanying international rules, it is less likely that these countries can exercise identical policies in the future. This has realized a

---

1. There eixsts a difference between Europe and the U.S. in adopting research networks. While European tendency was to concentrate on the National Innovation System influenced by the Brain Drain phenomenon during the post war period, the U.S. national labs have been isolated entities that were faithful to their original mission.

change of policy direction from Big business oriented industrial policy to a new focus on SMEs in Korea. A dilemma in promoting SMEs was that they lacked technological competitiveness (Kim, J 1999). Against the dilemma, networking the SMEs with research units is becoming a viable policy option, while more studies are required to test feasibility for a policy. This policy environment endows this research an opportunity to question feasibility of research network building in Korea.

## Theoretical Reference

With the background for building research networks, this research intends to find empirical data to support the feasibility of research network building in the Korea context. In doing so, this research finds theoretical reference on research networks from existing literature.

### *Definition of research network*

Research network can be defined as both formal and informal linkages among research and production units such as universities, research institutions, and firms that are connected to generate synergy while fulfilling their individual objectives (Freeman 1991; Debresson & Amesse 1991).

From existing studies, it is possible to find some necessary conditions that would generate research networks, which include implicit or tacit nature of knowledge and factors of trust that would enable the networks to be sustained. With these theoretical conditions, it becomes possible to infer conditions that would inhibit the development of networks in the below (Levy & Samuels 1991; Lynch 1990; NBIA 1997; Powell 1990).

- when participants to the network lacks experiences of Trust

- when there is no convergence on the long term goal among network participants

- when participants expect virtually no interactions in the future

- when there exists communicational difficulties in exchanging and learning knowledge & intellectual property

With the above conditions, factors of Trust, frequency, experience, Interaction seem to be the important variables that would enable or inhibit the formation and maintenance of research networks (Koschatzky & Kulicke 1994; Gibson & Rogers 1994; Hamel et al. 1989; Hipple 1987). Thus, in empirical survey to find feasibility of a more formal research networks, it would be crucial to investigate the above variables to the respondents.

## Methodology
### Data & Sampling Frame

In order to deduce the feasibility of formal research network as a policy option, this research utilized survey method to acquire data set. In doing so, it became crucial to define the sampling frame. Since this research aimed at research network between SMEs and government funded research institutions, thinking that this element would be weakest linkage in designing a hypothetical National Innovation system with currently available research resources, an important step was to narrow down the concepts and the scope of SMEs and researchers at the government funded research institutions or labs.

In defining the SMEs, this research selected SMEs that are technologically intensive and advanced. On this definition, the following argument can be suggested. Policy of building research network can be described as technologically intensive in nature, especially in the Korean context in which previous policies were mainly related to offering financing measures. (Galbraith & Kim 1998) This characteristic offers a clue in the sense that demand for this type of policy would mainly come from advanced SMEs whose competitiveness mainly relies on technology itself (Porter 1998; Rothwell 1984).

Together with the hurdle of refining the scope of SMEs, another important task of sampling SMEs came from their geographical and industrial distribution. This issue shows a seemingly biased sampling result which,in fact, can be justified, considering the context of a country where this research has undertaken. Since this research focused on advanced SMEs in Korea where certain industrial sectors have technological competitiveness in the world market such as electronics industry(Kim, J 2000), it becomes quite natural that advanced SMEs in that country would likely to emulate the industrial terrain of the mainstream industry.(Reid 1993a, 1993b). In the Korean context, it would be the electronics, communication and information related sectors. In other words, advanced SMEs in Korea, as of 1999 when the survey for this research was conducted, were predominantly in electronics and its related sector. Thus, while the survey tried to balance diverse industrial portfolio, the natural reflection of the SMEs' world itself is dominated by electronics related firms (see Appendix for the distribution of industries).

Similarly, those advanced SMEs in Korea tended to locate themselves(Reid 1993a,b) in Great metropolitan Seoul area where distance to downtown Seoul can be defined approximated 1 and half-hours. This is a justification for the seemingly biased sampling which in fact reflects the true distribution of the target industries under study. For the government funded research institutes, this research selected those labs located in Seoul and Taejon area, since these two regions hold most of the advanced research labs in Korea.

## Defining Researchers both at SMEs and Government funded Labs

In selecting the people who actually were surveyed, this research had a sampling scheme of asking researchers at both SMEs and research labs. The fact that SMEs under the sampling frame is advanced ones denotes that there are in-house researchers in those firms. For the labs, this research selected those researchers with Ph D. degree and previous experience with SMEs regarding technical consultations, assistance, or joint-research to check whether their experiences of informal network, which tends to be generated naturally, influence their support for a more formal network. The condition that researchers at labs should have previous experience of working with SMEs dramatically reduced the size of population itself available in Korea. This decision, however, was thought to provide serious answers regarding the feasibility of network building.

With the ideas for sampling frame, this research surveyed 105 SMEs in which one questionnaire was asked per firm. For the labs, 102 Ph. D. level experienced researchers from three major government labs were surveyed.[2]

## Frame of Analysis and Research Methods

The overall scheme of this research starts with comparing the Korean case with the theoretical guidelines from the existing literature. Especially this research finds crucial variables reported by existing literature such as trust, long term nature of the relationship, frequency, and satisfaction with the existing relationship. Prior hypothesis in designing the research can be presented

---

2.  Survey questions for the SMEs and government labs overlap greatly, although the questions for SMEs are shorter reflecting their work loads and prior contacts that restricted the length of survey.

in Figure1. First, we can be sure that the crucial variables mentioned above has relationship with the development of informal network, which develops naturally. The causal link is that with the development of the crucial variables, research performance would be affected. Prior expectation is that as the crucial variables develop in a way to activate informal networks, and then it will improve research performance. This research asked whether previous experience of informal networking would strengthen the respondents' preference for a more formal networking policy to improve research performance (Schrader 1991; Perrin 1988; Debresson & Amesse 1991). In so doing, LOGIT regression was utilized to deduce the support for the networking as a policy option. If the Logit model proves to be statistically significant, it would offer an opportunity to compare the Korean case with the theoretical hypothesis whether the four crucial variables are important in the Korean context. If the four variables or a certain combination of the four turn out to be meaningful, it would imply that successful formal networking policy would depend on "healthy" informal networking". This would illuminate the direction networking policy would be forwarded.

## Logic of Critical Case Study

In proposing the research design, it is also important to prepare for validity of research. In other words, it would be helpful, if this research design can persuade audience on why case study method in survey is meaningful. For this, it is possible to refer an influential forerunner in this tradition, namely critical case study method by John Goldthorpe (Goldthorpe 1968,1969). His contribution was an offspring of his research question: "would increased wealth change attitude of blue collar workers in the 1960s in Britain?" In actualizing his research, his research design was to find the most industrially advanced region of Britain, which was Lutton, to test his hypothesis. His logic was that if the hypothesis is rejected in Lutton, where workers' attitude is most likely to be changed, the hypothesis is very likely to be rejected in all other industrial regions of the country. Thus, the case study method is virtually applying the logic of statistical testing, especially hypothesis testing.

This idea can be broadly applied to this research. After defining the focus of the research on the research network between advanced SMEs and government labs, the critical case study method offers this research a justification to defend the geographical & industrial concentration in Korea, due to the country's specific context illustrated in the previous section (Kim, J 1999).

## Logit Model

The previous section presented that this paper utilizes important variables that are crucial in forming networks. To fulfill the purpose of the research, this paper employed Logit modeling to deduce the feasibility for a formal networking policy between SMEs and government labs. In the below, it is possible to present the Logit models used for Labs and SMEs. Due to minor differences in survey format (lengths and questions), specifications differ, although they eventually quest for the identical question.

## Logit model for Government funded research institutions

In designing the Logit model, dependent variable is the necessity for a formal research network expressed in response to a direct question asking the necessity, in which 0 denotes that it is unnecessary, while 1 denotes that it is necessary. For independent variables, this research employed years at work, age, frequency of cooperative research or interaction previously experienced with other firms and institutions, experience of trust from the previous cooperative research or interaction, and size of firms researchers worked with in the past. With the above variables, it is possible to present the specification as follows.

**Model 1-1:** Dependent Variable with a response from a direct question
**Necessity for research network (0= not necessary/1= necessary)= constant + years at work(X1) + AGE (X2) + frequency of cooperative research or interaction previously experienced with SMEs (X3) + experience of trust from the previous cooperative research or interaction (X4) + firm size (X5)**

## An Indirect measure for the support of Network

In model 1-1, dependent variable was the necessity for a formal research network as expressed in a direct question. A concern with this was the skewness of answer toward the support for the network as a policy option. To verify the original specification that it is decent and to resolve the possible problem, this research had a built-in shadow question asking essentially the same content. The intention was that if the two specifications show similar results, it would strengthen the validity of the model.

**Model 1-2:** Dependent Variable with a response from an Indirect direct question

Necessity for research network (0= not necessary/1= necessary)= constant + years at work(X1) + AGE (X2) + frequency of cooperative research or interaction previously experienced with SMEs (X3) + experience of trust from the previous cooperative research or interaction (X4) + firm size (X5)

## *Logit for SMEs*

In the SME case, dependent variable is also the necessity for a formal research network, in which 0 denotes that it is unnecessary, while 1 denotes that it is necessary. For independent variables, years at work, age, frequency of cooperative research or interaction previously experienced with government funded research institutions, satisfaction level for the current government policies and experience of communication efficiency from the previous cooperative research or interaction were employed. Due to differences in survey format, trust variable was not utilized, but the communication variable works as a proxy in the sense that it works as a determing variable to support the network.

With these variables, specification for SMEs' logit model can be presented.
Model 2 (SMEs)

Necessity for research network (0= not necessary/1= necessary)= constant + years at work(X1) + AGE (X2) + frequency of cooperative research or interaction previously experienced with SMEs (X3) + satisfaction level for the current government policies(X4) + experience of communication efficiency from the previous cooperative research or interaction (X5)

## Results from Logit Regression

### *Research Institutions*

From Table 1 in the below, both model 1-1 & 1-2 showed their statistical significance. In both models, except for the variable, age(X2), all other variables' coefficients showed identical directions, which convinced the validity of the model. As will be explained, the difference in direction found in age variable can be attributable to the difference in the way the question was asked, whether it was a direct or an indirect one.

The main implication from the result is the re-confirmation of the theoretical arguments on the importance of the pivotal variables in building and maintaining the networks, namely trust and the frequency of cooperation. In addition, the model presented implications from other variables including work years, age, and the type of firms researchers worked with.

**Table 4-3: Logit Results from Model 1-1(Research Institutions with Direct question)**

|  | Const.B0 | WKYRS | AGE | CO_RE | TRUST | FIRMSIZE |
|---|---|---|---|---|---|---|
| Estimate | -2.61633682 | 0.02274619 | 0.11353236 | 0.55926377 | 1.3349179 | -0.94487494 |
| Antilog |  | 1.023 | 1.12 | 1.7493 | 3.79969 | -2.57249 |
| Chi-sq=12.478 | P=0.02881 | Loss Function: Maximum Likelihood | Final Loss: 32.675142576 | N of 0's:13 N of 1's:89 |  |  |

To interpret the meaning of the coefficients from the Logit model, it is necessary to convert the figures into plain numbers by taking "antilog" transformation. As the table shows in the antilog row, as one unit of age increases, which is ten years in the survey, the probability that a researcher would support the formal research network building increases by 12%. Work years, in which 3 years is an unit, shows a 2.3% increase of support for the network with one unit (3 years) increase of work experience by a researcher. The most influential variable, trust, presents a dramatic figure. As one level of trust in the 5 scale trust indicator increases, support for the network increases by 279%. Similarly frequency of cooperative research shows 74.9% increase with a unit increase in the 3 level frequency scale used in this research. A peculiar finding, which reflects the Korean context, comes from interpretation of Firm size variable. The result shows that co-research experience with "big" firms reduces the support for the network, which indirectly evidences that various factors in building network, including communication, did not work well with the big firms. This, reflexively, suggests that networking policy may be started between SMEs and research institutions, since researchers at the government labs showed low preference for the big firms.

**Table 4-4: Logit Results from Model 1-2(Research Institutions with Indirect question)**

|  | Const.B0 | WKYRS | AGE | CO_RE | TRUST | FIRMSIZE |
|---|---|---|---|---|---|---|
| Estimate | 1.59983861 | 0.05422311 | -0.89076012 | 0.02312133 | 0.69912601 | -0.88185245 |

**Table 4-4: Logit Results from Model 1-2(Research Institutions with Indirect question) (Continued)**

| Antilog | | 1.0557 | -2.4369 | 1.0233 | 2.0119 | -2.415 |
|---|---|---|---|---|---|---|
| Chi-Sq=11.685 | P=0.03939 | Loss Function: Maximum Likelihood | Final Loss: 62.727838356 | N of 0's:42 N of 1's:59 | | |

In model 1-2, similar interpretation can be presented, except "age". To begin with identical results, trust,work years together with frequency of cooperative research marked important variables in support of network in the order from the most influential one. With one level increase in the 3 scale trust indicator, support for the network increased by about 101%, while with a unit increase of work years (3 years), 5.57% was increased. Frequency of cooperative research showed smaller coefficients, which reflects its reduced impact. Firm size variable also showed similar direction, compared to its role in model 1-1. In comparison, a highlight can be given to the "Age" variable, which presented a coefficient in the opposite direction. With one unit of age (10 years) increases in model 1-2, about 143% decrease for the support of network occurred. In interpreting this, it is possible to mention that the indirect question used in model 1-2 may have revealed the hidden preference for the network related to age factor. Thus, it is reasonable to infer from the results in model 1-2 that relatively young researchers tended to favor the idea of building research network.

## SMEs

For the SMEs, this research presents a single model, basically due to different survey environments. In other words, advanced SMEs tended to dislike long questionnaire, and this reduced the length of questionnaire utilized in the survey of research institutions. Despite this, overall, it was possible to retrieve broadly similar results from the survey and the model.

**Table 4-5: Logit Results from Model 2 (SMEs)**

| | Const.B0 | WKYRS | AGE | CORE | SATF | COMM |
|---|---|---|---|---|---|---|
| Estimate | -2.62455726 | -0.34318364 | 0.63421345 | 0.08345325 | 0.58712476 | 0.63139445 |

**Table 4-5: Logit Results from Model 2 (SMEs) (Continued)**

| Antilog | | -1.409 | 1.885 | 1.087 | 1.799 | 1.88 |
|---|---|---|---|---|---|---|
| Chi-Sq= 13.733 | P=0.0174 | Loss Function: Maximum Likelihood | Final Loss: 73.6413 | N of 0's:32 N of 1's:130 | | |

In the SME model, as mentioned in the above, communication variable was designed to act as a proxy for trust variable. This variable was the most influential variable in the model by having the highest coefficient. With a unit increase of communication indicator, support for network increased about 88%. In comparison to the model for Government labs, the importance of the work years and age variables expressed in the magnitude of coefficients is noteworthy. With a unit increase of age(10 years), support for network increased by 88.5%, while work years variable showed reduction in support for network by 40% with a unit increase of work years(3 years). The direction found in work years is opposite to that from the government lab models. People at advanced SMEs had a tendency to favor network with increase of age, while showed disfavor for it as they accumulate work years.

*Policy Implications*

From the analysis in this paper, it is possible to infer the following policy implications.

First, it is the rediscovery of the importance of informal network. Existing theories have told us the importance of those variables such as trust and frequency of interaction in the formation and maintenance of network (Levy & Samuels 1991; Lynch 1990; Hipple 1987;Hamel et al 1989; Gibson & Rogers 1994). This research confirmed the salience of these variables in the settings of research institutions and SMEs. What is more important regarding this finding is the possible link between basic elements of network building and feasibility of network as a policy option.

When basic factors conducive to the development of informal network, research performance was enhanced, which was reported in the survey of this research. When this experience, i.e. link between conducive conditions for network and enhanced research performance, is experienced, researchers both at government labs and advanced SMEs showed clear support for the research network as a feasible policy option.

Second, from the finding regarding the importance of informal network, it is reasonable to argue that a policy option to promote formal research network can be found meaningful only when informal networks can be maintained. In other words, maintenance of informal networks can be regarded as a sufficient condition that enables formal network as a policy option.

Third, technology trading, for example, can be regarded as a type of policy available within the umbrella of formal research network that can foster the development of informal networks by increasing "traffic volume" of research needs at both government labs and SMEs. Therefore, it is reasonable to argue that there are mutually reinforcing relationship between informal and formal research networks. And it would be the role of a government policy to make the first link between the two.

Through the survey and research, this paper has presented the dynamic of research networks. Despite the fact that this research setting was in Korea, it is quite reasonable to infer generalization that can be applied into the relationship between firms and research labs in other regions and countries. The most important implication from this research is an insight on how to foster informal research networks so that these can be functionally workable with more formal research networks that can be proposed by government policies. Results from this paper showed that strengthening the basics of informal networks such as trust and frequency of interaction is the keystone(Hipple 1987; Hamel et al 1989;Gibson & Rogers 1994;Levy & Samuels 1991) in starting the research network as a policy option.

As a concluding remark, it is possible to mention the salience of this research. As we have reviewed in the first part of this paper, networking has been widely accepted as the way to enhance research performance. The trend has been expressed in various forms and levels from macro level National Innovation system to science city and business incubators at micro level all over the globe. What is salient in this paper is to approach a micro foundation in building the research networks at various levels. Also, as the final word, this research tradition would greatly benefit if an analysis can be carried out on an international basis.

# 5

## Targeting the Future

### Introduction

Digital economy is a new key word describing a new facet of our economy as opposed to the existing traditional image of the economy (Tapscott 1995,1999). While different conceptions of the digital economy exist, it is fair to discuss the boundary of the digital economy that forms a common ground. First, the term digital economy is used to describe both equipment-manufacturing sectors and service sectors that utilize the digital equipment. Second, it is also reasonable to argue that digital economy can not be conceived as a discontinuity from the existing old economy, composed of manufacturing and service sectors (Kim, J 2002).

This chapter, with the backdrop, takes a position to understand the digital economy as the economy in which economic transactions are performed with digital technology (Cortada 2000, Tapscott et al. 2000), by which position manufacturing sector of digital equipment is regarded as the "infra structure" that sustains the digital economy from supply side; in comparison, household consumption can be regarded as the component of demand side "infra structure". With this conception, this paper attempts to analyze the supply & demand side development patterns of the infra structure of the digital economy in Korea between 1989 and 2000 with the Bank of Korea's data in order to present the dynamic that brought the growth of digital economy with an eventual aim to draw some implications.

# Growth of Digital Economy in Korea
## *Policy measures for installing the Digital Infra Structure*

Among diverse groups in business and academia, it may be a common thinking that there exist separate and distinctive policy measures suited for the IT sector. Against this easily perceived idea, there is no specifically designated policy measure for the sector, when one approaches the core mechanisms of policy measures.

As presented in table 5-1, policy measures for industrial promotion can be divided into two groups, incentives and regulation, which can be applied to virtually every industrial sector for all governments. Among incentive policies, it is possible to distinguish between policies of monetary incentives and those with non-monetary incentives. Policies of monetary incentives are, in fact, known to take the lion's share when one discusses the contents of industrial policy in many countries. Inside the umbrella of industrial policy of monetary incentives, there is a quite wide spectrum of policies, ranging from tax credits, finance to demand creation and infra structure building including social infra structure (Lee 1996). Among them, tax incentives and finance measures are regarded as controversial in the sense that these policies may distort the economy with the "visible hands of government"(Kim, J. 2002, Norton, R.D 1986). Separate from the theoretical debate on its harmful effects, this type of policies have been in practice in many developing countries including Korea (Kim, J. 2002, Galbraith and Kim 2001). It is also a common finding that as an economy develops in its size and mode of governance from government-led to private sector-led, direct measures of industrial policy are reduced in relative terms (Sakong 1987,Galbraith and Kim 1998). Regarding IT sector promotion, if a country's policy is linked to annual investment of the country, it would be fair to understand that the country's policies include incentive policies of monetary nature.

### Table 5-1: Universal Tools of Industrial Policy

| Incentive Policies | 1. Monetary Incentive Policy |
| --- | --- |
| | -Tax holidays |
| | -Financial Incentives (low interest rate, long term credit) |
| | -Demand Creation Policies |

**Table 5-1: Universal Tools of Industrial Policy (Continued)**

-Social Infra structure provision

2. Non-Monetary Policy

-Vision Statement policy

-Competition policy

-Consortium policy

**Regulation Policies**  1. Monetary Regulation

-Credit line control

-Tariffs

2. Market Entry policy

-Permission

-Anti-Monopoly and Oligopoly policy (anti-trust policy)

In comparison, policies of demand creation and social infra structure building are clearly less market distorting than the other type of incentive policy. One thing to note, however, is that in utilizing demand creation policy, financial capacity and mechanism of a country determines the extent of the policy in that country. For example, limits of credit lines allowable to firms and households are examples that demand policy can be operated within. In promoting IT sector in Korea, the Korean government has wisely utilized the demand creation policy. An earlier example of this policy is found in the case of personal computer industry promotion in the early 1980s, at which time the Korean industry was in its infant stage. The way the policy worked was that the demand creation was made by making educational needs of students. At this time, a policy example was to host computer skills contest for elementary schools students whose parents were forced to expend on PCs. After the initial promotion, IBM compatible PCs were in great demand for teenagers through the 1990s.

Non-monetary incentive policies include "vision statement policy" (Norton, R.D. 1986), building cooperative networks (Kim, J 1999), and promotion of competition. The vision statement policy is valid in the sense that private sector receives the direction of the government in the way the government will manage the economy in the future. Building cooperative networks have been widely in use, as exemplified in SEMATECH and numerous consortium schemes in Japan (Kim, J 1999, Anchordoguy 1988). In the promotion of IT sector, this type of policies were also in great "demand". In regulation policies, market entrance regulation has been a very strong policy tool of government including the Korean case. As was the case in other sectoral promotion, regulating the number of firms has been in practice in cellular phone service market, which can be an example of the policy (Kim, J. 2002).

In sum in this section, it is reasonable to argue that policy measures that have been effective in other sectors have also been in use in IT sector promotion in Korea, which forms the infra structure of the digital economy. In the next section, this paper will review the industrial performance of the IT sector in Korea as expressed in published data before going into analyzing the growth of IT infra structure in Korea.

### Industry performance: An Overview of Current Status of Digital Infra Structure in Korea

As discussed previously, this paper understands the digital infra structure as the manufacturing sectors that produce equipment of digital technology, namely communication equipment and computers. This section reviews the development track of the digital infra structure industries in Korea during the period this paper is aiming at.

As known to many different layers of audience, Korea's semiconductor industry, mainly memory chip production, has had great competitiveness. This paper, however, excludes the sector in its scope of digital infra structure to faithfully focus on the impact of policies on the digital manufacturing sectors. As it will be discussed with analytical eyes, Korea's digital infra structure has seen a fast growth during the 1990s.

### Communications Equipment sector

In Korea, from the late 1990s on, communications equipment sector saw a dramatic increase of portion taken by cellular phone production. This sector, however, is composed of more than just the cellular phone production. It includes switching system and related sectors including routers and cable manufacturing. During the 1997–2000 period, the sector has experienced a growth of 25.2% in terms of production volume, 7.7% in its value adding, 49% by the standards of export volume, and 17.5% increase in the number of firms (Statistical bureau of Korea, Manufacturing & Extraction Statistics Report, each year). It is also noteworthy that the sector's portion in terms of total manufacturing sectors has remained as minimal. Statistics show that the percentage of communications equipment manufacturing & related firms among total number of manufacturing firms has marked 1.4% in 2000 by having 1,360 firms among the total of 98,110 manufacturing firms, which is a modest growth from 0.9% in 1997.

Viewing from a global perspective, Korea's digital infra structure as seen in communications equipment production has also recorded a significant growth as with China, as seen in table .5-2.

**Table 5-2: Profile of Communications Equipment Industry** [*]

|           | 1997   | 1998   | 1999    | 2000    | 2001   |
|-----------|--------|--------|---------|---------|--------|
| Country   | amount | amount | amount  | amount  | amount |
| U.S.      | 94,638 | 96,287 | 108,676 | 123,761 | 99,471 |
| Japan     | 40,983 | 33,392 | 39,561  | 46,855  | 49,356 |
| France    | 14,589 | 15,745 | 16,447  | 17,672  | 15,801 |
| Korea     | 6,200  | 6,004  | 11,530  | 17,078  | 15,370 |
| China     | 6,100  | 7,400  | 9,300   | 12,700  | 15,279 |

[*]   (Source: Reed Electronics Research, Yearbook of World Electronics
      Data, Each Year ; Unit: Million U.S. Dollars)

As presented in table 5-2, the U.S. production volume clearly showed the country's relative economic down turn, especially the high tech sectors during the year 2001. Another conspicuous finding is that the growth of China and Korea that now show equal proportion in the world production vis-a-vis that of France. Still interesting to observe is that production volume in Asia showed a relatively healthy growth, especially with the cases of China and Korea, while the proportions France and the U.S. took has shrunken. According to the Reed electronics research data, during the 1997–2000 period, the world communications equipment market has grown by 11.2% on average, which suggests that if a country's growth in production is higher than the figure, then there must be some plausible causes or scenarios that brought the outcome. As will be explained in the Korean case in this paper, the working of an industrial policy measures can work as a leverage to actualize the growth above the world market trend.

*Computer Manufacturing sector*

Computer manufacturing industry in Korea has been mainly composed of personal computer manufacturing sector with some segments of server class computers. During the 1997-2000 period, this sector has marked a growth of 26.7% and 11.2% in terms of production volume and number of firms respectively. In contrast, however, it is noteworthy that this sector has shown a decrease of employed workers by 3.4% in the same period, which shows a degree of automation and modular assembly of parts vis-à-vis other manufacturing sectors. By the standards of production volume, this sector took approximately 4.4% among total manufacturing production volume (Statistical Bureau of Korea each year). The number of firms has been increased from 460 in 1997 to 632 in year 2000.

Looking from a global perspective, the world PC market size has been reported as 40,000 units in 1981, which has been increased to 114 million units n 1999. In 2000, it was reported to reach about 132 million units globally, which was reduced in 2001 to 125 million units (Korea Association for Electronics Industry Promotion 2002). In table 5-3, it is possible to see the proportion of PC production and market distribution over the world.

### Table 5-3: Proportion of PC production and market distribution [*]

| Proportion(%)/Region | U.S. | Japan | Asia | Europe | others | Total |
|---|---|---|---|---|---|---|
| Production | 24.1 | 17.4 | 34 | 14.9 | 9.6 | 100 |
| Market Distribution | 33.8 | 16.6 | 13.8 | 24.7 | 11.1 | 100 |

\* Source: Reed Electronics Research, The Yearbook of World Electronics
Data 2002.

From table 5-3 and other information, it is possible to get several implications. One is that Asian countries have been production bases for the world
PC industry, while the U.S. and European countries import those PCs produced overseas (Senyo 2002). Second, it is also interesting to know the com-
position of Korea's PC industry. According to industry statistics, about half of
Korean PC production volume is exported as shown in Table 5-4.

### Table 5-4: Market Structure of Korea's PC market *

|  | 1997 | 1998 | 1999 | 2000 | 2001 |
|---|---|---|---|---|---|
| Domestic Produc-tion(A) | 9,631 | 7,619 | 13,163 | 17,572 | 14,518 |
| Export (B) | 5,320 | 4,669 | 7,267 | 9,531 | 7,672 |
| Import (C) | 2,294 | 1,470 | 3,122 | 5,110 | 3,989 |
| Domestic Consumption (A-B) + (C) | 6,605 | 4,420 | 9,018 | 13,151 | 10,475 |
| Ratio of Export among Domestic Production | 55.2% | 61.3% | 55.2% | 54.2% | 54.2% |

\* Source: Korea Association for Information and Communication Industry
Promotion 2002
Unit: Million U.S. Dollars

Third, PC production and demand for PCs are turned out to be sensitive to
economic fluctuation (Brynjolfsson et al 2000, Liebowitz 2000). At the same
time, the fact that PC production and demand have risen in 1999 from a
slump in 1998 implies that demand promotion and creation as a policy would
work, as it will be analyzed in the later part of this research, which can be exercised as a momentum for the recovery of the economy.

Fourth, it is reasonable to comment on the status of the Korean PC industry in terms of its position. That is, in contrast to the regional characteristic of

Asia as a whole, Korea's PC industry has been more attuned to domestic market. Of course, with the statistic of nearly 50% of production volume going into export market, one can still argue that the sector is export oriented, but looking at the figure in table 5-4 that the ratio of export to total regional production in Asia is 2.46 : 1, it is arguably correct to present the Korean PC sector as domestically oriented one. One way to understand this comes from the fact that there is no major PC production firm or brand in the world market, compared to other Korean electronics products or Taiwanese PC brands with production line in China. Researchers have attributed to this as a misfit between Korea's corporate governance system and the characteristic of PC market and technology development trend (Shy 2001). In other words, Korean firms have been at their best at mass production and economy of scale oriented manufacturing even in electronics sector such as semiconductors[Kim, J 2002], while weak in adapting to fastly moving PC market, which required more sensitive moves in flexible manufacturing style which Taiwanese firms proved to be agile (Harrison 1994).

## Data & Method

This research utilized the Bank of Korea's Statistics on production Index of industrial sectors from 1989 to 2000 and final consumption expenditures of households between 1993 and 1999. This research employed a set of cluster and discriminant analysis applied to time series data to find out time series natured determinants that have shaped the growth pattern of industrial sectors with an aim at finding the development pattern of IT sectors to analyze whether they would form infra-structure for digital economy with the case of Korea.

Previous research utilizing time series tuned cluster and discriminant analysis has employed wage data to present how economic determinants have molded wage performance, and thereby presented economic policy meaning of the determinants (roots) with the case of Korea and international comparison (Galbraith & Kim 2001, Kim, J. 2001). Succeeding the core contents of the methodology used for wage analysis (Kim, J. 2002, Galbraith & Kim 1998), this research tried to expand the envelope of the methodology by using a different time series data to reveal the determinants structure embedded within the data. Since the methodology has proved that it can discover the underlying economic forces from times series data, it is reasonable to argue that the methodology can be applied to economic time series such as production index in this research. While industrial production index is utilized to present "supply" side of the digital infra structure, in this research final household expenditures by accounts were used to evidence a partial but empirical side of "demand" side aspect of the digital infra structure.

## Analysis of the Digital Infra structure in Korea: Findings
*Cluster Grouping : Supply side*

The aim of cluster analysis in this research is to find a structure of industries based on similarity of cumulative annual change rate of production index. In comparison, in the demand side cluster analysis, the variables of interest are the different consumption accounts to find out a distinctive consumption pattern. Time series based cluster grouping in this research has produced a two group structure, as shown in Figure 5-1. The grouping structure shows a similarity of annual growth pattern of the industries which is the supply side backbone of the digital economy in Korea.

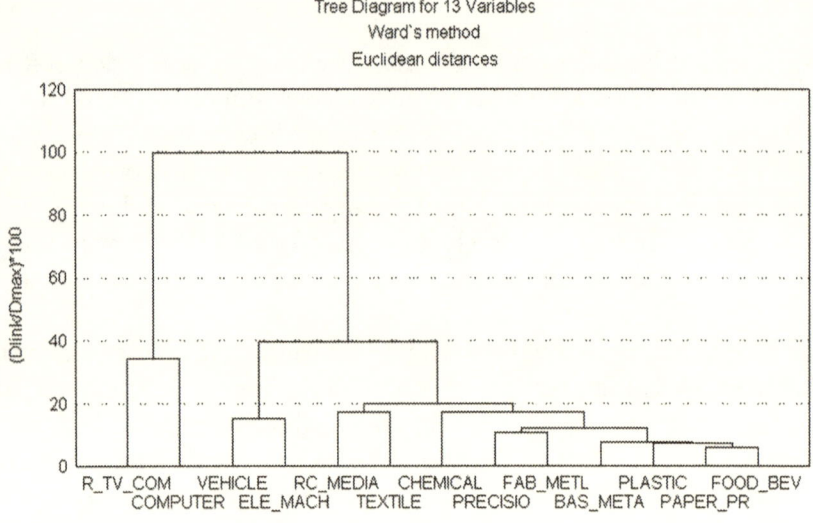

Figure 5-1 Cluster diagram of the digital Infra structure in Korea 1989-2000 (supply side)

From the grouping, the left hand side group with computer and communication equipment is the infra structure, which clearly shows a distinguishable growth pattern compared to traditional sectors.

## Demand side

As discussed in the preceding section, Korea's industrial promotion of IT sectors also came in the form of demand creation. This has, in turn, been interpreted as the participation of household expenditures in IT related service sectors. In the Korean case, 1990s saw a tremendous growth of mobile telephone and broad band high speed internet services at home, which can be traced through Figure 5-2.

In Figure 5-2, Communication account, among household expenditure items, has placed itself as a distinctive group vis-à-vis other expenditure items and thereby proved that it functioned as a demand creation measure in the IT sector promotion.

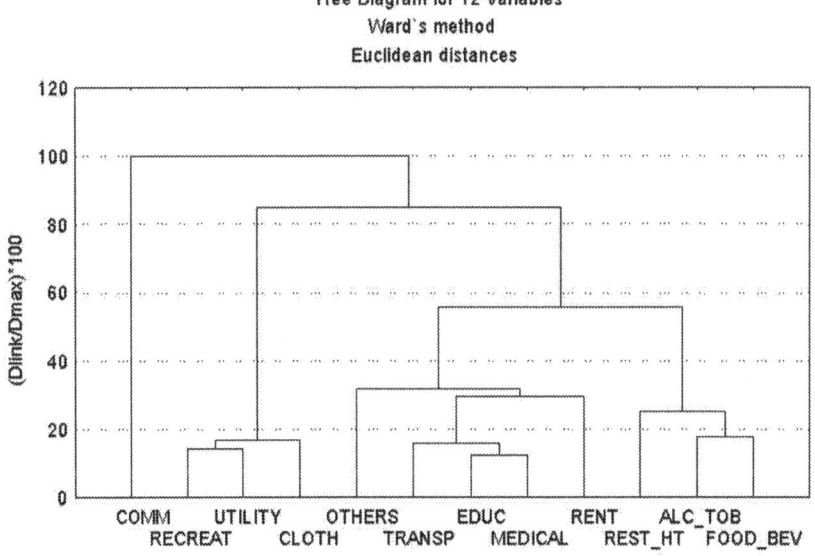

Figure 5-2 Household expenditure growth pattern (1993-1999)

Index:: Sectors and Expenditure accounts in full expressions
Figure 5-1 : Manufacturing sectors

Group 1: radio, TV, and Communication equipment, Computer & related equipment

Group 2: vehicle, electrical machinery, record & media, textile, chemical, precision equipment, fabricated metal, basic metal, plastic, paper product, food & beverage

Figure 5-2 : Household Expenditure Items

Group 1: Communication Services (fixed line, mobile phone, broad band internet services, cable TV etc) ; Group 2: recreation, utility, cloth; Group 3: other expenditure, transportation, education, medical expenditure, rent; Group 4: restaurant/hotel, alcohol & tobacco, food & beverage

## Determinants of supply side Infra structure

The cluster structure yielded was utilized in time series tuned discriminant analysis in order to extract historical determinants that have shaped the digital infra structure pattern in supply side from 1989 to 2000 period in Korea. With iterative matching with various time series indicators, a determinant was found, which was turned out to be best matching with the root with historical meaning. Especially, in this type of analysis utilizing discriminant analysis, those roots were extracted by maximizing between group variance, and minimizing within group variance, following Ward's method (Ward 1963).

In this research, the two group structure yielded a single statistically meaningful root, which takes nearly 100% of total variance of industrial production growth for the period in this research. This root was best matched with the annual investment of the Korean economy (Kim, J. 2002) in the period under study in time series format, as seen in Figure 5-3. From the matching with the annual investment series, it becomes reasonable to analyze industrial performance of IT and non-IT sectors in the following section.

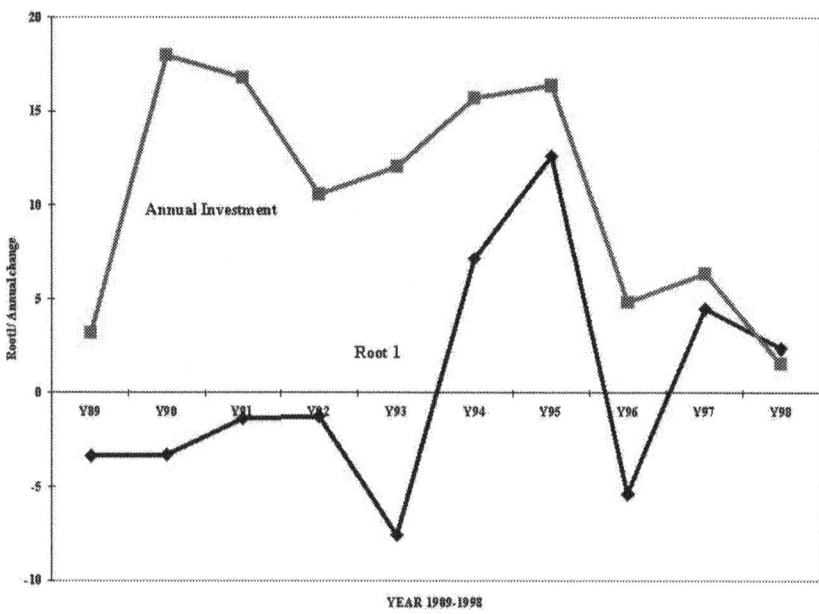

Figure 5-3 Annual Investment and the First Root Matching

## Interpretation of the Impacts of Policy Variable: Annual Investment

Analysis of the First Root

   After extracting the historical root that has shaped the growth pattern of IT and traditional sectors over the 12 years, it becomes crucial to analyze the impact of the discriminant root on both IT and non-IT(traditional) sectors, which can be explained with figure 4. Figure 5-4 shows how different industries can be located with respect to vertical and horizontal axes.

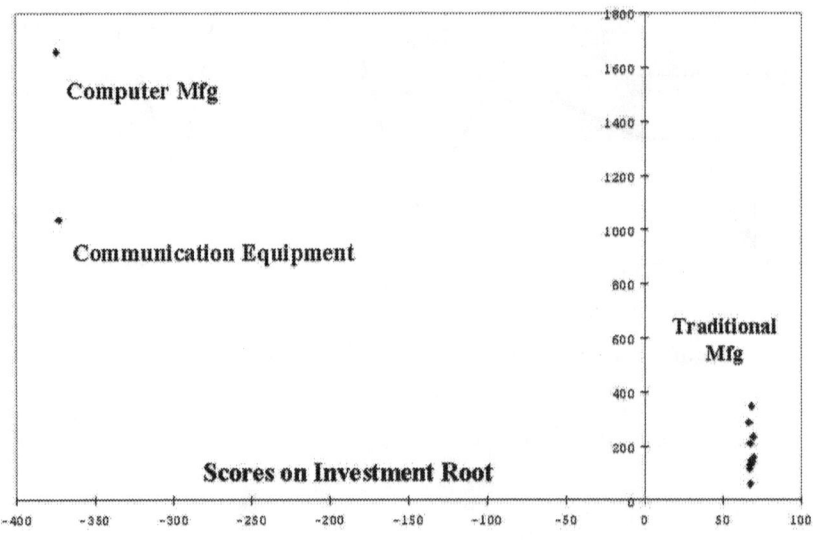

Figure 5-4 Annual Investment Root and the Cumulative Increase of Production Index(Vertical)

   In figure 5-4, the vertical axis is the cumulative increase of production index from 1989 to 2000 expressed in percentage, while the horizontal axis shows scores of each sector on the annual investment root. The cumulative increase of production for each industrial sector reflects the sector's general characteristics of growth during the 1989–2000 period, while the meaning of root one, the annual investment, can be approached by understanding the sensitivity of each sector to the root. In other words, scoring high on the first root means that when annual investment in Korea increases, a sector's sensitivity of industrial production is high. This implies that when a sector has a high cumulative growth with low sensitivity to the investment root, the growth of that sector should be explained with an alternative explanation.

Interpreting the figure 5-4 suggests the following points. First, it is reasonable to argue that the growth of IT manufacturing sector as the digital infra structure in Korea has been made independent of the annual investment pattern of the economy. This argument is made based on the finding that IT sector's score on the canonical root has turned out to be low. Second, despite the fact that IT manufacturing sector has been in disadvantageous position in relation to the impact of annual investment, the overall growth of the IT manufacturing sector has been tremendous by being grown over 1000 % during the 1989–2000 period(1,037 % for communication equipment and 1,659% for computer manufacturing sector respectively), in contrast to the traditional manufacturing sectors which grew only between 100 to 400 % during the same period.

As mentioned earlier, this "seemingly unusual" growth pattern should be explained with an alternative way, which is through the mechanisms of different policy tools. As with other manufacturing sectors, it is undeniably true that Korea's IT manufacturing sector has received government's attention. Despite the common point, what has made the IT sector's growth pattern so unique is found in that not only supply side (investment) policy but also demand side policy has been utilized and made effective with a heavier weight & efficacy on the latter as a hindsight in interpreting the results from this research.

As discussed, in the earlier section, policies of industrial promotion includes demand side promotion, and in the Korean case household and service sector demand for IT sector products in a broad sense has brought the phenomenal growth of the IT sector. This is all the more eye-catching in the sense that IT manufacturing sector marked a sharp growth even when Korea's investment was sluggish after the 1997 financial crisis. Thus, it would be fair to claim that government's general policy to boost the economy through consumption has found an "exit", the IT sector, to buy more "manufacturing products, which marked the gigantic growth of the IT sector with the Korean economy's transition by being coupled with the IT technology.

Of course, if one is determined to list all the policies of demand creation and non-monetary incentives, it would be possible even to present citizens' PC policy[1] in 1999 or government's directional policy for high speed network providers[2] in the sense that the policies worked as vision making. It would be, however, more important to recognize the efficacy of demand side policies vis-à-vis supply side promotion policies which has widely been used in the Korean soil.

## Implications
### *Financial Aspect of the Dynamic*

From this case, two implications can be gleaned.

Conventional understanding & research findings on the Korean economy have mainly centered around what government has done to develop or promote a specific sector in the economy (Amsden 1989). Thus, one can also argue that Korea's IT manufacturing sector as the backbone of the digital infra structure in Korea has also been a subject of government's promotion. There is, however, a subtle but significant difference in understanding the development of the IT sector. That is, while the development of most industrial sectors in Korea has been performed with supply side policy measures, which include monetary and non-monetary incentive policies that aim at increasing & creating production capabilities, the IT sector promotion has been practiced with demand creation approach. This difference has to be understood with a broader angle on the Korean economy.

As most audience would recall, the Korean economy has experienced an economic crisis since 1997(Hong 1999), which resulted in changes of the ways the Korean government can promote industries and necessities to boost the economy. In fact, even before the crisis and independent of the economic crisis, the Korean government's move to promote an industrial sector has been "limited" by the WTO agreement on Subsidies and Countervailing Measures which describes no direct subsidy to an industry. Together with the existing limits imposed by international regimes like the WTO agreement, policy

1.  The Korean government has implemented a policy to provide a low cost citizens' PC with aims to spread the use of internet services and also to boost the PC industry. The target price of the machine was lower than what industry has expected. So only venders that they claimed they can meet the price zone participated in the program, and the machines were available through postal offices.
2.  The Korean government also wanted to install high speed internet networks in 1990s, at which time industry expressed objections due to their fear for low demand. Government's directional policy, vision making, to invest and create markets in high speed networks gave industry business confidence.

measures to meet economic crisis found a solution from a boost of the domestic economy.

As explained earlier in this paper, the boost was found in diverse ways including policies to "buy" more IT products & services. To enable this, government and the central bank, The Bank of Korea, allowed commercial banks to make loans approval to households and personal loans easier. Also put into practice was to increase credit lines for personal loans and credit cards owned by individuals.

## *Policy Mechanism*

As the second implication, it would be meaningful to note the financial aspect of the dynamic. As mentioned in the preceding segment of this paper, increasing "credit availability" to households & individuals provided a necessary condition to purchase more IT products and services (KDI 2001). Despite the "fulfilled" condition, it is noteworthy that it was households that eagerly purchased "durable" goods including cars, PCs, high speed internet services, and cellular phones with the increased credit. Firms had relatively little appetite to invest in IT products and services vis-à-vis households due to relatively decreased annual investment with the economic crisis.

That is why, in Figure 4, the performance of IT manufacturing sector in Korea showed a very distinctive pattern by showing high growth rate independent of the dynamic of annual investment pattern. In other words, IT manufacturing sector in Korea, especially during late 1990s and early 2000s marked a phenomenal growth even when annual investment growth was weak, due to strong demand creation. This is understandable with a logical sequence that the increased credit line was, first, used to buy more durables including IT products, which, then, had a spill-over effect to overall economy.

## Possibility for generalization

It is also possible to infer few points regarding the possibility for generalization with the case of installing digital infra structure in Korea. First, it is not all new to find that demand creation was used to boost the economy from a slow recovery. Since the New Deal era, it has been an often used policy measure. Like the characters in the Wizard of OZ, who symbolize the Great Depression of 1930s, households in Korea in 1990s were left in the downturn of the economy. Like the characters were restored in the novel, the Korean households clearly contributed to the revival of the economy with their spending from increased credit lines.

Second, there is, however, another point to recall in understanding the recovery of the Korean economy and IT sector growth. On this, it is important to be reminded that Korea's electronics sector was "out-there" to receive the shower of demand. If there were no such sector with preparation, in a counter-intuitive sense, it would have been difficult to expect the growth of IT manufacturing as the IT infra structure in Korea.

Third, it is arguably interesting to point out that one of the critical reasons to "invite" the financial crisis of 1997 has been government—controlled banks. Despite the crisis, the phenomenon of government dominance has not waned out as one infers from the findings from the recovery of the Korean economy. As mentioned, government guided a policy to increase credit lines and commercial banks allowed more personal and household loans. In this process, it is important that government, through the central bank, could exercise more than interest rate policy could do. At least one evidence was found in a move in the fall of 2002 to recover ill-managed household loans without changing interest rates. Thus, it would be a point of academic discussion in times to come whether a national characteristic would remain or how long would it take to change a national tradition of government dominance in managing the financial sector.

Fourth, it is also meaningful to note a side effect of the demand creation policy backed by credit line expansion. As one can imagine, some of the loans turned out to be ill-managed debts, while credit card & cellular phone issuance to teenagers created ill credit problems to those subscribers. In fact, ill managed loans have more to do with real estate market speculation. Compared to this, building IT manufacturing sector as the digital infra structure is worthy of being called as a policy success with its contribution to the recovery of the economy.

# 6

# Globalization of the Public Sector: A Social Capital Perspective

## Introduction

With increasing trend of globalization in every sphere of life, it is nearly impossible for us to think in an isolated way as past generations had done. Started mainly from private economic areas(Ohmae 1990; Kim, J 2001), globalization has started penetrating into areas where traditionally national and regional peculiarities were respected (Farazmand 1999, Malcom 1995) and therefore no such thing as global standards can be discussed.(Korten 1995; Cox 1993) These areas include cultural spheres and more sensitively the areas of the public sector in which traditional concept based on sovereignty seems impossible to co-exist with the globalization and global standards themselves (Cheung 1997).

With this change, it is not unnatural these days to discuss the globalization of the public sector (Wilson 1994). In the context of this book, regional development, the role of government is so crucial to be overlooked, not because it is the only institution, but because it can affect the formation and maintenance of social capital, which can be regarded as the soil in which policy effects can be produced. With this understanding, a special focus is given to the analysis of civic & social culture and its foundations in Korea in analyzing the possible origin of the lacking development toward globalization in Korea. With the preceding discussion, this chapter will carefully suggest a future direction for improving public sector globalization in Korea.

## Why is social capital important?

### Robert Putnam's usage of Social Capital

In this book, the author Robert Putnam "revives" the civic culture approach which was fully developed in the 1960s in Political Science in the behavioralism era. Civic Culture has been a major explanatory variable in persuading audience on the outcomes of a political system. On this foundation, what Putnam added was to link this prior foundation with his concept of "social capital" which he brings in from historical roots. The concept of social capital is Putnam's major determinant that produces divergence of institutional performance across southern and northern regional governments.

In developing his argument that areas with "rich" social capital, i.e. areas that have conducive environments for democracy and effective government, Putnam relied on several methodologies. First, in data gathering stage, he utilized panel data by asking the same group of people in his survey. Also he prepared various basic indicators which can be used as variables in his later analysis to produce composite indices. Second, in the analysis, he resorted to factor analysis as the statistical method.

For example, one of his example of composite indicators, the institutional performance, was constructed by utilizing variables(basic indicators) such as reform legislation, day care centers, housing and urban development, legislative innovation, cabinet stability, industrial policy instruments, and local health unit spending. For all these variables, factor loadings were calculated, and for a region's performance, these variables or basic indicators were added after by being factor loadings are multiplied to each variable.

After finishing this job of making a composite index of institutional performance, Putnam relies on "correlation" figures with other variables of interest; one example is correlation between civic community and institutional performance. With these correlation figures, he contrasted the difference between the south and the north. His analysis mainly stops at this stage, and in chapter 5, he traces a possible causal diagram.

## Critique

Despite the fact that this book is written with elaboration, still there is room for criticism. First, by resorting to historical roots back into medieval periods, the author is making deterministic conclusion.

Second, in a narrow time frame, Putnam also presents that civic involvement in the 1900s had strong impacts on both civic involvement in the 1970s and economic development in the 1970s; with these two variables of the 1970s, he derives institutional performance of the 1980s in Italy. I suspect a missing link here. Although Putnam did not put an arrow between socio economic development in the 1970s and civic involvement in the 1970s, there must be a strong impact from the socio economic development to civic involvement. Thus, I argue that Putnam mis-specified his model.

Then, how can this be convincing will be my next point, which I will briefly touch on. What I think is more convincing is a maturation along the industrialization. Above all, as industrialization takes place in the north, people moved from south to north following their opportunities; these people must have been most able-bodied people in the south and there likelihood of having "modern" civic value would be very high. A consequence is the even more depletion of civic social capital in the South. With a similar logic, if industrialization had taken place in the south, civic roots may have changed. Thus, if we can immigration records from south to north from the 1900s on, we can approach a more convincing testbed for the "civic roots" argument.

Third, the fact that Putnam too much relies on correlation figures for his persuasion may be his weakness. Correlation can be just necessary conditions for causality. His study tried to overcome the limitations of case study method by increasing implications from various regions in Italy; but in addition to this, in my view, if he could add cases from other countries on the relationship between civicness and democracy(institutional performance), we can see whether the civic roots argument would have persuasive power.

### Salience in the regional development context

In the regional development context, social capital is an important asset. In attributing & analyzing policy success and failure in social science research, there has been difficult theoretical concepts that have tried to capture the essence of the cases. Concepts like collective action by Mancur Olson shows an example of how economic incentives can be structured in delivering collective goods, i.e. policy outcomes. The notion of path-dependency, for example, has presented how past legacies can constrain the course of actions & their outcomes. The concept implies that where social & economic foundation is functionally structured, there would be much higher possibilities of success, while in the opposite case, chances of failure are likely. While reviewing these concepts, it is possible to" eye-on" a fundamental notion that would encompass both economic & socio-cultural foundation that a society has or is endowed with. This notion brings this chapter to focus on the notion of social capital.

In using the notion, this chapter has introduced its reference from Robert Putnam's theory. Despite this, however, his book tries to capture even wider range in adopting the concept of social capital. Social capital would therefore be operationally defined as socio-economic and cultural heritage & endowments that work in policy mechanism. In some sense, this book wants to incorporate Michael Porter's notion of competitive advantage in discussing social capital, because in Porter's notion, competitive advantage can be created and improved, while in comparative advantage world, it is a destiny that would not be changed.

Turning the argument back into the regional development context, it is possible to exemplify with a hypothetical case. If there are two research complexes in the same region or a country that have practiced very similar policy tools, including policies with economic incentives, yet their performance were greatly diverging, there would be two ways to attribute the consequences. One would be focusing on firm behavior in each complex, while the other would be examing the "social" environments. If firm or industry behavior would be quite standard, the only attributable point would be the social environments. When looking at those success stories of the Silicon Valley or even classical cases of the third Italy, a way to "abstractize" the dynamic would be looking at the social environments, which this chapter calls the social capital. In treating social, cultural aspects in theory, there would be two approaches: Universalism and Particularism. In making arguments with the social capital, this chapter does not rely entirely on universalism. Despite this, however, this chapter on Globalization of the Public Sector clearly notes that in facilitating regional development, there are common factors of social capital to be equipped with to generate successful outcomes. These would include components of trust, co-operation and attitudes toward collectivity.

## Deficiencies in Social Capital

Continuing from the argument that the notion of social capital(Putnam 1993, 1995) provides clues for approaching the issue of global standards in Public Administration, this chapter relies on a six country comparative survey on citizens' attitudes on 17 elements (Gong-Bo-Cheau 1997) that can be regarded as components of social capital per se. Before elaborating selected components that are closely reflecting the status that social capital in Korea vis-à-vis other countries, it is possible to present a summary table on what elements Korean people featured functional & dysfunctional aspects of "social capital".

### Table 6-1 Conducive vs. Negative factors for Social Capital

| Conducive Factors for Social Capital | **Negative Factors for Social Capital** |
|---|---|
| Attitudes toward collectivity: toward "Nation" →Reflecting the Nation-State characteristic | Attitudes toward collectivity: Low Citizenship →Less cultivated citizenship |
| | Negative attitudes for individual level participation or community service |
| Strong curiosity for Neighbors' activities | Relatively significant distance among neighbors →Early Modernization level |
| | Strong Insistence on one's will |
| Consciousness for conserving goods | Low preference for used products |
| | Relatively Low job satisfaction |

### *Attitudes on Collectivity*

In general, one would think that Korean people are collectively oriented. With this perception, it is interesting to review the results from the survey. From the survey, indeed, Korean people marked the highest scores in overall scores for collectivistic attitudes. A closer look, however, reveals a different picture. Koreans showed a spectrum of results on different questions in this category. On a survey item, "What is good for a nation is good for myself"? Koreans showed the highest mark among the people in six countries, while on a survey item," public duties are more important than private matters" and "people in my country prioritize national interests over private interests", Koreans marked 4<sup>th</sup> and 6<sup>th</sup> among the six countries (Gong-Bo-cheo 1997:36). These mismatching results imply that while Korean are aware of the consequences of collective action as a functional and positive one, internalization of the value has not taken place.

This low attitudes on collectivity is indirectly presented by another survey item. In a question, the survey asked citizens of different countries which country has highest attitudes toward collectivity. Citizens of Italy, Germany, and U.K. responded Korea as the lowest marked country, while people in the U.S. and Japan marked Korea as the 5<sup>th</sup> and 4<sup>th</sup> respectively. Korean people has their own self assessment by marking themselves as 4<sup>th</sup> among the six countries. What can be implied is that from the Western perspective where collectivism lies on civil society formation (Cohen), Korean society is regarded as lacking civicness per se.

## Social Gathering with Neighbors and Community Service

Survey revealed that Korean people have strong curiosity on neighbors' issues, but at the same time showed relative distance in actual events. Table shows that Koreans showed the highest rank for their response on the survey list "I will always participate in community activities. Despite the seemingly positive side of neighborhood relations depicted in the above table, yet an opposite picture is found. In mentioning this aspect, a careful attention is required. In table, Korean citizens marked high among the six nations surveyed on overall community service items. Koreans marked especially high on items that are normative and less specific in nature (Gong bo cheo 1997), and this tendency is reversed as the survey items are narrowed down to individual level ones that ask willingness for action. On item "I am willing to donate money to social service organization" and "I am willing to donate my internal organs", participation has shrunken in Korea. This characteristic of the Korean citizens work as an undermining factor in maintaining civil society. People, while they are aware of normative values, they are hardly motivated when they are asked to participate at the individual level.

## Conflict Resolution

On conflict resolution, Koreans are found to be relying on measures that are not based on discussion and compromise. In the survey, Koreans were the people that were most likely to recourse on "force" when conflict situations arise by marking the lowest scores(highest scores means likelihood of resolving conflicts through non-forces). A very similar response was found to a question asking that "we are not good at reaching a resolution through discussion". Koreans marked the lowest. While Koreans "confess" that they are not good at resolutions, Korean people clearly showed their normative values rooted in harmony and congruence. This also suggests a hint that there exists a gap between normative values to reach a congruence and the actual behavioral patterns in everyday lives, which in turn, provides a source for the discrepancies mentioned in the previous section among the three different conceptions of public sector performance. While social capital is known to have effects in mitigating conflicts in a community, the Korean context was far from this possibility.

Protection of civil rights is an important indicator by which one can diagnosis the character of a specific society. Compared to the citizens in other advanced nations, Korean showed relatively low marks on questions such as "Our government protects rights of people well" and "In my country, minority opinion and rights are well received and protected". An interesting contrast is also found in this survey item in the sense that there exists a dramatic difference exists between what people think as "just for themselves and what they can actually get in that society. Korean people, while they evaluated their society as not protecting their civil rights sufficiently, they clearly presented that they try to gain what is just for themselves in the realm of civil rights. On the survey item that "I try my best to get my rights as a consumer", Koreans marked higher than Japanese citizens.

On the survey item "I protest when I am mistreated at government offices", Korean and Japan marked relatively low vis-à-vis citizens in western countries. Similarly on a question list" I try to confront with government's wrongful policy", citizens of Korea and Japan showed relatively low marks. From a western point of view based on the notion of civil society, these two questions clearly reveal that these two Asian countries have relatively weaker tradition of civil society in the sense that citizens are not willing to express their grievance to their creature, the government. Another interesting finding was that Korean people were more likely to resort to news media including newspapers to express their dissatisfaction known to the public than citizens of other countries. This can be understood as a release mechanism of the dissatisfaction. All together, from a modern political theory's point of view, it would be fair to say that Korean society has weak foundation for civil society, as expressed in the survey items.

A dilemma is found in reviewing the two previous survey items, protection of individual rights and conflict resolution. The dilemma is that Koreans have normative value that there should be harmony, while there are dissatisfaction and conflicts among people and between citizens and government with virtually weak mechanisms to reach sound and peaceful resolutions per se. Furthermore, this dynamic can be aggravated with vicious cycles.

This chapter understands vicious cycles as conditions that increase tensions. For example, modernization and economic development,and political democratization all increase the satisfaction level of people, while there are no systematic social rules and glues to traffic-signal the issues and conflicts. This is the social soil from which Korean society is rooted and where public policy is implemented.

## Deeper Structure

Through the preceding section, this chapter has presented how Korean society can be compared with other societies in terms of survey items that can constitute proxies for estimating social capital. As one reviews the results from the survey, an explicit observation is that Korean society has on the surface seems to have benign elements that can lead to the accumulation of social capital. On the other hand, those elements are rooted in such a way to work against the formation of social capital.

Then, a natural question would follow on what does the deficient social capital have to do with the realization of global standards in the public sector in Korea? A critical answer to this question comes from a notion that social capital is the soil or foundation from which all social relations can be established. More specifically, government activities are materialized in the settings of a specific society, and conditions of social capital would condition the environments in which those government activities can be exercised (Fox 1996). Furthermore, it is crucial to acknowledge that activities of the government are made by making contacts with the private sector (Harriss 1997). Thus, if certain conditions in the private sector feature degraded nature, it will be transferred to the public sector naturally. A consequence would be the low public sector performance and frustrations from citizens' side. In this context, rule of game would be to "cheat", as would be exemplified in corruption cases. Also, all the efforts to improve the government would present only limited success, since the working environments are not favorable to the reform design.

## Differences in the formation of civil society

Now, with the link between social capital and public sector performance, our focus should be given on what may be the cause for the low social capital in the Korean society that eventually reduced public sector performance. In analyzing the deep structure, a clue comes from the origin and formation of civil society in Korea vis-à-vis that in western societies. From modern political philosophers including Hobbes and Locke, what has been the core in designing a political entity was the understanding of human beings as rational, weak, but at the same time harmful without some form of governing mechanism, in which check and balance was an important mechanism. Upon the philosophical foundation, liberals have introduced the role of groups, which has passed up to pluralists in the 20th century.

In comparison, the Korean society shows a different historical track in which civil society formation was not similar to that of typical western societies. The Korean social context can be characterized as inheriting traditional & authoritarian culture mixed with modern elements. A peculiar aspect is the advent of modern elements, which had no chance to build up civil society from the individual level.

Then what is the salience of the difference in understanding global standards in public administration and public policy? The difference brings a huge hiatus between typical western societies and the Korean society in design and implementation of public policy. In typical western societies, economic incentives are widely applied in order to change behavior or interaction patterns. From this, it is fair to argue that one can trace Hobbesian rational individuals even from a very modern "Rational Choice theory" or "Rational Choice based institutionalism" Thus, in terms of fitness, economic incentive based policy design dovetails with societies with well developed civil society tradition, while a society without it would feature a maladaptation in the sense that it would be difficult to expect an identical policy effects from the identical policy design used in western context. Ignoring this difference has often attributed a policy failure as i) a policy failure due from a simple emulation of the best practices in other countries, or ii) failure unknown origin, which increases a puzzle why certain policies would not work in Korea.

Following from a point that Korean social capital per se can be composed of the existing and traditional culture which is authoritarian and characteristics of civil society without individual orientation, what makes matters complex is the traditional social setting also had high moral density, by which it means a great degree of inter-dependence among the Korean people. This was expressed as people's great curiosity about neighbors' activities, while this curiosity could not be linked to social capital formation. As Korea gets modernized, organized interests tend to develop with weak individual level foundations mentioned earlier. This offers a source for increased difficulty in designing public policy suitable in the Korean soil.

Against the social settings, efforts to improve the government has mainly been focused on I) enhancing internal management and ii) improving service provision. While these two are essential in improving government, with respect to satisfaction by general citizens, these areas would provide marginal increase in satisfaction, since bigger chunk of conflict frontier comes from the areas outside the focused areas mentioned above. This can be attributable to why gaps have been existing among the Korean government, international institutions, and the general public regarding their views on public sector performance.

## Current Status and Achievements towards Globalization

### *An International Comparison*

As interests on globalization being increased, international efforts to understand different degrees of globalization has taken place (IMD 1996, 1997; WEF 1997). Despite their validity still being questioned in terms of methodology, including reliability of questionnaire and sampling frame, they still offer a good starting point to research globalization and its impact on diverse aspects of private and public sector. Among diverse surveys of its kind, one of the most well known report has been published by IMD.

The list of indicators include overall competitiveness scores for each country, and specific sub-items for both government and the private sector. For example, the government related indicators include support for business, small government, market orientation, and budget related indicators, while overall scores of government in international comparison are well known to general public.

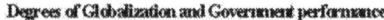

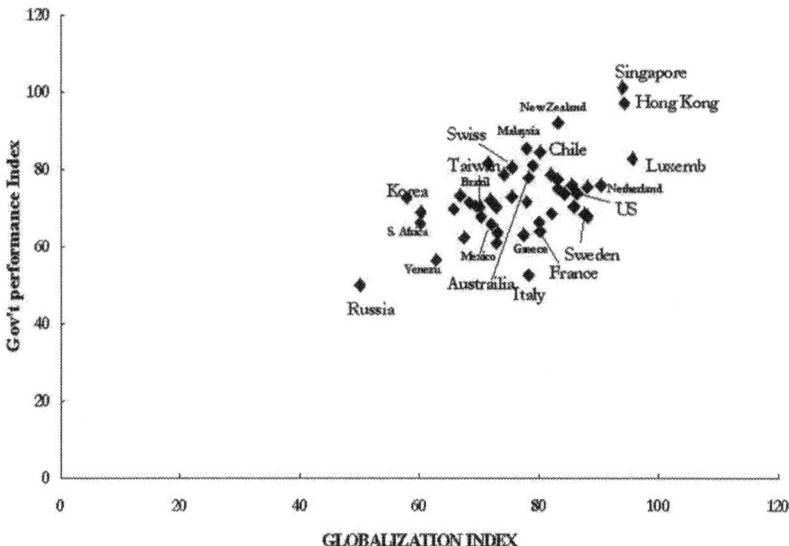

Figure 6-1 Globalization and Government Performance
(Source: Korea Economic Research Institute, Global Competitiveness of the
Korean Economy).

Figure 6-1 shows the plotting of globalization index and government performance index for 46 countries. The data is based on 1996 IMD report and
Korea Economic Research Institute (KERI)'S Global Competitiveness index,
with which this chapter re-processed to present an overview that there exists a
relationship between globalization and government performance index. From
the figure, it is reasonable to argue that in general, so called advanced nations
feature higher marks on globalization and government indexes. This suggest a
possibility that there "is" or possibly "may be" a tendency or trend regarding
the globalization of the government sector, assuming that advanced countries
still have something that developing countries should learn.

## Domestic Efforts to improve the Public Sector as harbingers towards Globalization

The preceding section of this chapter presented a status report by utilizing existing report on globalization. What was evident from the "picture" was that there is a direction toward which government sector can be improved, although actual dimensions of improvement for each country should be addressed in detailed efforts (Cheung 1997; Welch & Wong 1998). The impression from the IMD report has been that countries like Korea was not an impressive performer in overall indicators. Especially the government sector was marked lower than its private sector counterpart. While the report has been cited widely in Korea, questions regarding the validity of the evaluation method has always followed the citations. This offers a counter-intuitive question regarding what has been done in the improvement of public sector in Korea. In this section, this chapter will review the efforts undertaken by the Korean government so far to improve government in international standards.

### Earlier Efforts

Scholars broadly agree that the discipline of public administration and its application influenced by the U.S. was first introduced in Korea during the early 1960s. It was the hay day for comparative politics focusing on developing countries (Riggs 1964; Heady 1979), and this trend was imported in Korea in the name of comparative public administration and development administration. While assumptions lied in these theories are controversial by today's standards, it is reasonable to argue that these became the harbingers of modernizing the public sector towards global standards per se in the Korean society. Since its introduction, the discipline of public administration and its application has continuously influenced the public sector in Korea.

### An Assessment on recent efforts

From the 1980s on, efforts to improve the government has developed in mainly four directions, which can all be considered as efforts to level the Korea administration up to the global standards. The first one was a continuing tradition of improving the public management of government (Osborne & Gaebler 1993; OECD 1995). In this direction, recent developments include performance based pay system and open and contract based recruiting of civil servants, which reflect a philosophical change in managing the bureaucracy

(Kim, L 2000). Furthermore, in the public management side, the Korean reform has taken a path to incorporate more 'management-like' content in running the government. In this direction, a number of public functions were privatized or in the process of transition toward it (Price 1994;OECD 1993). Government's contracting out was also a similar effort to reduce the size and attain the goal of improving the management. Another management-like reform was the introduction of the agency system developed from the British tradition (Cheung 1997) to introduce business-like atmosphere where feasibilities are known at least theoretically and from foreign cases.

The second tradition in improving the government is found in improving service provision by government. The importance of improving service provision in the government is that it is the most frequent contact point by citizens vis-à-vis the government, where the government's efficacy is being contested (Lipsky, M 1980). Knowing this, the directions for improving service provision in Korea has started from reducing the waiting cues in the 'regional' field office (Dong-Sa-mu-so), reducing difficulties in issuing public documents, including passport, and reforming government regulations closely affecting ordinary people's lives.(Committee on Administrative Reform 1994) These efforts were greatly enhanced with the introduction of information technology in the public offices.

An important development in this area was the adoption of service charter in the late 1990s (Joo 1999). Following the British tradition, government offices in Korea established the service charter in which they defined the expectation level that general citizens can have in the service provision (Joo 1999).

Another critical development in understanding the public sector reform in Korea is the anti-corruption efforts, which are related to both the first and the second categories of efforts. Alarmed by the recent international surveys that placed Korea as one of the notorious country for corruption in the government, the anti-corruption efforts are one of the hot areas where attention for government reform is concentrated on (Office of Government Policy Coordination 1999).

The third area of improving government is policy evaluation. Despite the limited application of diverse methods & approaches, policy evaluation is a growing field where improving government is working. The fourth area is the emphasis on research. Compared to the old tradition, this is a significant change in policy thinking. To serve this, research institutions funded by government has undertaken a wide range of research projects that can be implemented in the government.

To sum up, the embryo to improve the government has been accelerated by two irreversible trends: One being the ever-increasing globalization, and the other a more recent wave came with the 1997 financial crisis that imposed an additional thrust to launch government reforms (Kim, L 2000).

## Discrepancy

In the preceding section, this chapter has reviewed the current status of globalization efforts by the Korean government and survey results by an international institution. The juxtaposition of the two trends, i.e. reform efforts to enhance the level of public administration and lagging performance surveyed by the international organization present a cleft to be analyzed. The cleft can be described in two dimensions. While the first gap is the one of perception in understanding the level of Public Administration between the Korean government and international institution, the second gap is the difference between the level of social capital and the development of public management in Korea.

This chapter argues that these gaps provide clues on why three parties, international organization, the Korean government, and general citizens in Korea, are all dissatisfied with their perception of globalization in the public sector. As shown in Figure 1, as for the Korean government, with its continuing reform activities from the past, it may think that the level of public administration has been greatly enhanced, while international institutions, such as IMD, has been presenting survey results quite opposite to the Korean government's expectation.

From the perspective of this chapter, a clue in understanding this discrepancy comes from the notion of "social capital"(Putnam 1993) endowed in the Korean context. As a consequence of the existing "social capital" in the Korean context, what we observe is the gap between relatively advanced public sector management and slowly changing social capital that dramatically undermines the efficacy people feel about public sector performance, since social capital level offers sufficient condition for the low perception.

# What to expect from the Government: A reflection from previous government reform

## Caveats with the NPM

Through the 1980s and 1990s, governments in the advanced economies have been pressed to accept 'business-like' atmosphere in governance. In government reform field, the new world-wide 'New Public Management' (NPM) paradigm (e.g. Hood 1991) has widely been understood to fit into the larger thesis of global convergence. The rise of NPM followed the privatization boom of the 1980s and is being entrenched in a philosophy of governance very much geared towards market-oriented reforms and reconfiguration (Aucoin 1990; Hood 1991; Lan and Rosenbloom 1992).

The use of the economic market as a model for political and administrative relationships; A similarity in the goals pursued and the technologies utilized by each reform movement; and The use of administrative technologies such as customer service, performance-based contracting, competition, market incentives and deregulation (Kaboolian 1998: 190).

The OECD has considered the globalization of public management principles and practices to be part of a broader globalization process (OECD 1996). In this line of thinking, it was assumed that the globalized economic and informational contexts have facilitated an international exchange of ideas and policy options, so that "governments can draw on experimentation in other countries in the process of defining their own policy responses" (OECD 1996). Summarizing the 1990s situation, OECD, however, had to admit that while member countries' reform strategies have many points in common, "there is no single model of reform, there are no off-the-shelf solutions" (OECD 1995: 25). Differences among countries are seen in the emphasis and take-up of particular reform initiatives. There existed important divergence in reform objectives, with some countries setting a reduction in the size of the public sector as a major objective while others focusing on improving the performance and strengthening the role of their public service (OECD 1995).

Even with some common stories on the emergence of NPM measures, not all OECD countries had moved to adopt NPM principles to the same extent during the 1980s, and marked differences existed even within the same 'family groups' of countries (Castles 1990; Hood 1990). Reviewing global public sector reforms (Cheung 1997),it is possible to admit national diversity. Even among OECD countries, significant diversities were observed in terms of the style, focus and locus of NPM-style reforms. Anglo-Saxon countries tended to favor reforming their public service, but continental European countries emphasized decentralization.

For example, while New Zealand and UK concentrated on 'agencification' and 'managerializing' their core public services, Germany left the style of its public service largely intact and instead focused its attention on the creation of private-law companies outside the boundary of core government and the read-justment of administrative functions and financial responsibilities between the federal and Lander governments. The scope of British privatization was broader because there existed more nationalized industries, whereas in Germany Volkswagen and VEBA had already been privatized in the 1960s and Lufthansa was a private-law company from its inception (Derlien 2000). Also many local water and electricity supply or transport enterprises no longer had public law status in Germany when UK began its privatizations. Privatization only occurred in a large scale in Germany during the 1990s when the east German state economy was privatized following reunification. Other countries like France, Australia and New Zealand did not make privatization the key to their public sector reform program. In the US, where state-owned industries did not exist, the emphasis was on the de-regulation of private enterprises.

All of these evidences clear suggest that there should be national character-istic in designing government reform, even in the case one can admit that there exists a "global trend".

### Agnecification: A hard landing case from Korea

Modeled after the British government's executive agency system, the Korean government's reform agenda during the 1998–2002 period included the 'agen-cification' (Yoo & Kim) of its government offices. In actualization, each min-istry has designated at least one office to be the independent agency. Under the MOST(Ministry of Science & Technology), the Korea Meteorological Agency (KMA)[1] has selected its aeronautical meteorology section as the office for the agnecification. As known from the British case, about 17% of total rev-enues from cost recovery in the U.K. meteorology case comes from the avia-tion part (Yoo & Kim). In the Korean case, unlike the U.K. case in which the

---

1.  The KMA itself, although includes the title agency, is not a British style agency.

whole MET(weather service) has become an agency, only aeronautical meteo-rological function has become the agency.

To prepare the cost recovery scheme, several researches were conducted. A cost benefit analysis provided the direct costs to serve the aviation meteorology at airports and related research. In the calculation, due to relatively low wages of public sector employees vis-à-vis its private sector counterparts, the direct costs were understood about 5% of the total KMA budget in year 2000. Despite this low figure, to have a genuine cost recovery structure, it was neces-sary to have a full cost structure in processing & analyzing the data. To fulfill this purpose, indirect costs were calculated, which was about 9% of total KMA budget. Thus, one could approximately infer that the total estimated costs to produce & serve the aviation community was about 14% of total KMA bud-get. Considering the fact that the British MET's portion from aviation part is about 17% among its total revenues, which includes about 7-8% of profits in it, estimates from the Korean case seemed quite reasonable.

In actual practice, the KMA has taken a partial recovery scheme through its long policy deliberation process with airlines, which resulted in recovering the direct costs part, which is a cost recovery scheme aimed at collecting costs to run the avian meteorology offices only. This has left a fundamental problem of partial recovery.

The unresolved problem is that if partial recovery is geared toward recover-ing direct costs only, which is the sum of wages and organizational manage-ment costs for the aviation meteorology office, where would funding sources for replacing the equipments come from. An assumption in the partial recov-ery plan is that heavy budget required equipments like radars would be funded still be the central government. If this condition is what the partial recovery is aimed at, then one can criticize that the partial recovery is a crippling idea from the beginning, not fulfilling the original policy idea to reduce financial burdens of central government and thereby attain the government reform pur-poses.

If one can have a rosy expectation that full cost recovery is possible, even in this case, there is a danger of actualizing the cost recovery plan. When full cost recovery is feasible, the 'price for the service' would be hard pressed to meet market competitiveness, which is in functional relations with aviation indus-try's profitability. This will naturally indicate that the recovery rate will be determined as low level as possible due to airlines' bargaining power. If this will be manifested, the next sequence will also be the financial shrinking for the budget for replacing expensive equipments. Thus, it would be a reasonable conjecture that neither partial nor full cost recovery will guarantee funding for replacing the equipments.

But, there is an even more serious problem. Replacing equipment in the above paragraphs has assumed purchasing equipment with similar capability or equipment with int'l development trend at best. What if, however, a country wants to upgrade its meteorological technology by having a newer and bolder technology based equipment, which is linked to spending more money? This will not be feasible under the recovery scheme. An implication is that once recovery scheme is put into practice, introducing new technology will also be checked, due to the logic that introduced the recovery. This dynamic will again reduce possibility of introducing new scientific and technological findings into practice, as long as money matters (Yoo & Kim 2005). In sum, cost recovery scheme will make us to re-ask what would be the role of the public sector, which will clearly suggest that one should have clear understanding when using cost recovery scheme.

### Foreign Best practices: Its efficacy and limitations with the case of New Zealand

For many people, the case of New Zealand as the best practice for government & public sector reform has been seen as the universal model that can be applied to other countries. This is the very reason why foreign best practices should be carefully reviewed & wisely adopted. The New Zealand way of reforming government has been famous for its faithful application of market principles in reform. Not only in reference model, but also in practice, the people of New Zealand has actually put into practice what the books have described about their reform.

In understanding the reform, however, it is quite critical to note in what context the country had to adopt the "market" based reform. New Zealand has been a prosperous country since the late 19th century. April of 1882 gave a landmark to New Zealand for the first export shipment of frozen meat. With refrigerating technology used to carry frozen meat to the Northern Hemisphere, together with countries like Argentina, New Zealand could enjoy the inflow of incomes. The country's stance in the world economy continued to be strong when the price of world woolen products was in hike in the 1950s, when the country marked the country with the 10th largest per capita income. The recipe for success also gave a cause for the decline of the country. Due to heavy reliance on sheep and its byproducts, the country's economy could not benefit from the expansion of the world economy with the explosion of trade among countries.

If a country is sufficiently large, like the U.S., limited dependence on trade can be bearable. If a country heavily relies on trade and its products have limited capacity to add values continuously, the country is about to be a "price-taker". New Zealand was exactly the case. New Zealand could not enjoy the expansion of trade volume. While most other countries could increase their GDP, this island country had to take relatively lowered price, if the demand conditions for its products turned out to be unfavorable. Looking at domestic side of New Zealand, the country seemed to be in good shape. Its ratio of public expenditure among GDP was less than 45% at the highest moment, which was lower than those number of Belgium, Denmark and Sweden. Furthermore, New Zealand has been under the protectionist trade policy and capital control, though the level of capital control was milder than France, Italy, and Scandinavian countries in the 1980s. Thus, it is reasonable to argue that the momentum for reform came from the country's acknowledgement of its "Business Model", i.e. its trade structure vis-à-vis its trade partners.

## Regarding the Downsizing practices of the New Zealand case

While the Business model argument presented shows a larger background to evaluate the New Zealand style reform, a more detailed argument can be presented regarding the Downsizing practices of the New Zealand case of its public sector. Based on a case from the Port Authority (Corporation), it is possible to distill a critical ceiling through which government downsizing should not pass. As seen in Figure, most organizational structure seems to have a hierarchical shape. Despite all the blames the shape might get, one of the undeniable merit comes from its capacity to coordinate departments from one level higher. In the New Zealand's port corporation case, while maintaining the shape, a clear exception was observed.

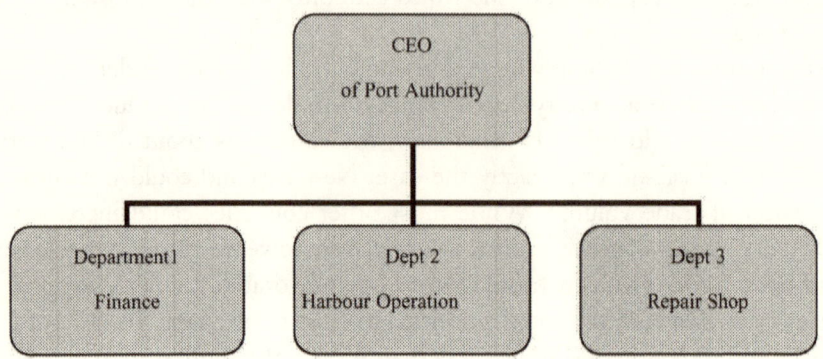

Figure 6-2 A Simple Organizational chart to explain reform

According to researchers on organizational issues, one critical advantage of making an organization is to reduce "transactions costs" among the functions, which in this case, represented by departments. Without organizing efforts, these departments could have been independent entities. In the New Zealand case, by following the market principle at organizational level, the internal transactions among & between departments were reformed to be "cash-based". Thus, without cash transfers first, maintenance department would not initiate its repair missions. A careful reader would instantly get the meaning. Though fashionable in some Management theories like the Business Process reengineering(BPR) theories, pushing the public sector reform to this ceiling would make the existence of an organization to "void". If the reform drives the transactions costs up, then the organization is "dead". There is no necessity to "share" the same roof of the organizational title. This does not mean that reform in New Zealand was wrong in the country's contexts, but, at least, it implies that there exists a critical limitation in generalizing the New Zealand style downsizing of the public sector.

It was this context that New Zealand has decided to thoroughly "mar-ketize" its public functions. New Zealand's society as a whole had a consensus that its export sector is critical to the survival of the country. Thus, the philos-ophy of the reform, while taking Hayekian in theory, in actual terms were to minimize the logistics costs for exports. From harbour and port authority to government offices, the Hayekian reform was the agenda. This leaves a quiet, but fundamental repercussion to the audience of the New Zealand's reform. As long as one of its audience country is an exporter of raw material with no or limited chances of adding values, the New Zealand approach may seem rational. By contrast, if a country has a production portfolio made up of value adding products, the minimization of social support functions and streamlining based on the market only principle is an alternative with irrevocable sacrifices of the other sectors. It is this context that foreign bench marking cases should be examined before being applied, and also the global scale New Public Management(NPM) does not mean that individual national characteristics of reform should be underestimated.

## A Concluding remark: Social Capital Enhancing Policies

This chapter has started from a discussion on social capital on why it is important. With an international comparison on social capital, this chapter tried to present the spectrum of the issue, i.e. the relationship between policy effectiveness and the status of social capital. Then a review was presented in what has been the government reform in Korea, followed by caveats from the recent government reform activities. The Korean case was used as an exemplar that can hold possible implications for other countries. As a closing to this chapter, it is possible to mention that government policies related to regional development should be social capital enhancing policies in order to produce not only desired policy outcomes, but also a series of unintended but functional consequences.

In actual and individual cases of each country, the meaning of social capital enhancing policy would mean different things. Despite the divergence, however, there is one common element that the discussion on social capital can inspire. That is, a simple idea or a formula style approach to "install" or "transplant" foreign best practices, including the construction of science & technology parks and research networks, would turn out to be either a policy failure or a very inefficient policy, if social capital element is not considered seriously. In this regard, so far as the functions of the public sector matters in a society, the degrees of government and public sector competitiveness would make great differences in economic & industrial performance of regions and countries.

# 7

# Conclusion

Through preceding chapters, this book has discussed seemingly different thematic areas. Under the apparently distinguishable topics, however, lies a common thread, which is the role of government in the changing environment of globalization. Especially this book has devoted its discussion on the role of government in economic development beyond the traditional roles of government presented in chapter 1. As discussed, in many countries, the types of policies government can exercise have converged, as mentioned in chapter 1, in the areas of promotional and regulation policies.

What this book has been trying to inspire was that the areas & roles that government can & should exercise would be different in the contexts of today & tomorrow. This is not to deny the "structure" of policy tools that government has utilized so far. Rather, the change implies that the role of government should be refined to meet the challenges with the 'identical' policy tools. Part I of this book has provided the contents for this change. As shown, major industrial sectors have presented an ever-intensifying trend of globalization.

The evidence for globalization presented in this book is two folds. First, it was clearly possible to deduce cluster structure based on time series characteristics of wage data, which works as a 'genuine' proxy for industrial performance. In the grouping structure for industrial sectors under this study, all sectors have shown grouping in line with familiar economic blocs such as EU, NAFTA, and others. Without this kind of empirical analysis, the formation of economic blocs would seem as a mere political rhetoric based on incipient movement toward economic integration. A better and closer approach to the analysis presented in this book would present single industry case studies or trade structure analysis of a specific economic zones. In the view of this book, previous approaches can only provide partial evidence vis-à-vis multi-spectral façades of the real world. With cluster structure for each selected industry, this book has tried to present the accumulated trend toward the formation of economic blocs and globalization.

The second evidence that part I of this book has provided as evidence for globalization comes from the notion that greater portion of industrial & economic performance has been affected by a single or only limited number of key economic variables in time series, which has been turned out in this book as the U.S. money supply changes. The fact that the portion explained by the U.S. indicator has increased signifies the deepening of economic integration at the world level. Also impressive has been that except for some industrial sectors, most of the sectors studied in this analysis showed that they have been affected by the U.S. money supply.

Against the backdrop of analysis presented in part I, part II of this book has presented an array of new roles of government. All of the policy measures have a common purpose or a rationale in that these policies were designed to overcome the reduced efficacy of the existing policy tools of government in boosting economic performance. Despite this common thread, there exists a spectrum among policies presented in each chapter of part II. Building research networks, as presented in chapter 4, and research clusters presented in chapter3 clearly are examples of policies to be widely applied in both advanced & developing countries. In contrast, chapter 5 clearly would find its audience in developing countries where aiming at a group of high technology sectors really means something.

Despite the range of policies that varies in audience, there is a clear message to be transferred from chapter 6, which is an explanation on so called social capital notion for policies. Without decent deposit of social capital in a certain society or country, it would be more than inefficient to just pour in resources for R&D and economic development. This does, not, however, mean that the notion of social capital would bring a deterministic interpretation for countries, for it is quite likely that certain unique social capital types would tend to stay over time for that society. In a sharp contrast to the common interpretation, this book is more inclined to suggest that a society or a country would apt to find a better fitting policy types and mechanisms to the social & economic environments of that society or country to have a better economic as well as prospective R&D performance.

# APPENDIX

## Cluster Analysis and Discriminant Analysis on industrial wage data: Procedures in Mathematical Illustration

Step 1: Average Wage Rates

Begin with an NxT matrix **R** of average wage rates(or comparable performance variable) for N officially-defined industries for years t=0 to T. (3 digit SIC codes are typically used.)

Step 2: Convert to Time Series Data

Convert to an Nx(T-1)=NxP matrix **G** whose elements $g_{it}$ are the rates of change of the performance variable for i=1 to N industries for years t=1 to T. Each row g is therefore a time-series of rates of change.

Step 3: Clustering Method

Cluster the rows of **G** according to the Euclidean distance $D=\sqrt{(_t(g_{it}-g_{jt})^2}$ criterion using Ward's method(a hierarchical agglomerative procedure that minimizes within-group variance relative to between-group variance at each step).

## Step 4: Grouping

Choose an appropriate level of grouping based on the agglomeration schedule and marginal loss of information as clustering progresses. That is, stop clustering at **K** groups when the algorithm starts forcing dissimilar objects into awkward and unwieldy clusters.

## Step 5: Discriminant Criterion

Consider the P-dimensional matrices **B** and **W**, where the diagonal element of **B** is the variance between groups for each year t=1 to T, and the diagonal element of **W** is the within-group variance. The problem is to find the P-column vector a such that $a'Ba/a'Wa=\lambda$ is maximized. $\lambda$ is the discriminant criterion.

## Step 6: Eigen Vectors

The solutions to the above problem are found by maximizing the discriminant criterion, eg:

$$(W^{-1}B-\lambda I)a=0$$

Each eigenvector $a_i$ is a root ("canonical root") of the discriminant function, associated with an eigenvalue $\lambda_i$, etc. The eigenvalues may be ranked by size. The original element in this analysis consists in nothing that the eigenvectors, though usually considered as strictly as weighting functions or factor loadings, *are in this case themselves time series, whose elements are $a_{11}$ through $a_{1T}$, etc.* The eigenvectors thus measure the set of forces through time that discriminate between the performance (wage) behavior of groups of industries. There are K-1 eigenvectors, since $W^{-1}B$ has rank K-1.

## Step 7: Time Series Forces

Are these "forces" themselves economic variables? To approach this problem, we first compute the "canonical scores" for each group of industries. If we have a KxP matrix of these rates of change of mean wages by group, with time-series rows $g_j$, then compute: $a'_i g_j$, etc, for all eigenvectors and groups. Then, rank the groups by canonical scores on each eigenvector, and examine for clues as to the economic force responsible for discrimination.

Step 8: Iterative Matching

Search for a historical rate-of-change time-series corresponding to the force f hypothesized in the previous step. Plot and compare to the movement of the eigenvector.

(Occasionally, converting to index values and scaling is necessary.)

# Bibliography

Amin, A, (1999). An Institutionalist Perspective on Regional Economic Development, *International Journal of Urban and Regional Research*, 23(2), 365-378

Amin, A. & Thrift N.(eds.) (1994). *Globalization, Institution and Regional Development in Europe*, Oxford University Press, Oxford.

Amsden, Alice (1989) Asia's Next Giant: South Korea and Late Industrialization. New York and London: Oxford University Press.

Anchordoguy, Marie (1988) "Mastering the Market" International Organization Vol 42(3) Summer.

Bain, Joe., Barriers to New Competition: Their Character and Consequences in Manufacturing Industries, Cambridge MA: Harvard University Press. 1956.

Balnchflower, David G, Andrew J. Oswald, and Peter Sanfey "Wages, Profits, and Rent-Sharing." *Quarterly Journal of Economics* Feb 1996 Issue 1. pp.227-251

Berger, Suzzane. (1981). *Organizing Interests in Western Europe*. Cambridge University Press. Cambridge.

Bergman, E and E Feser, (1999). Industry clusters: a methodology and framework for regional development policy in the United States, OECD, *Boosting Innovation*: The Cluster App roach, pp. 243~268

Boltho, Andrea. (1982). *The European Economy: Growth and Crisis.* Oxford University Press.

Boyer, R. (1988). *The Theory of Regulation.* (translation in English). Manuscript. Paris.

Boyer, Robert. (2001). "The Development of the Neoclassical Tradition in Labor Economics", *Industrial and Labor Relations Review,* Jan 2001 v54 i2

Brummer, Alex, "A Blow to the very Heart of Europe", *Airline Business.* Sept. 1993.

Brynjolfsson, Erik & Brian Kahin (Editors) (2000) *Understanding the Digital Economy*: Data, Tools, and Research MIT Press Cambridge, Mass.

Bulmer, Simon, "Domestic Politics and European Community Policy Making", *Journal of Common Market Studies,* Vol 21(1983).

Capello, R., (1999). "Spatial transfer of Knowledge in High Technology Milieu: Learning versus Collective Learning Processes," *Regional Studies,* Vol.33, No.4, 353-365

Castells, M. and Hall, P., (1994). *Technopoles of the World,* Routledge.

Cheung, Anthony B. L.(1997). "Understanding Public-Sector Reforms: Global Trends and Diverse Agendas". *International Review of Administrative Sciences.* 63(4). 435-458.

Cocks, Peter. "Towards a Marxist Theory of European Integration", *International Organization,* Winter 1980.

Committee on Administrative Reform (1994). *Road to Globalization.* (in Korean)

Conceição, P., Heitor, M.V., Oliveira, P.M.(1998) "Expectations for the University in the Knowledge Based Economy", *Technological Forecasting & Social Change,* 58(3): 203-214.

Cooke et. al., (1997). *Regional Innovation Systems* : Institutional and Organizational Dimensions, Research Policy, 26

Cooke, P., (1992). *Regional Innovation Systems* : Competitive Regulation in the New Europe, Geoforum, 23

Cooke, P., (1998a). "Global clustering and regional innovation: Systematic integration in Wales," in H. Braczyk, P. Cooke, P. and M. Heidenreich, eds., *Regional Innovation Systems*, 245-262, UCL Press,

Cooke, P., (1998b). Introduction: Origins of the Concepts, in *Regional Innovation Systems*, Braczyk H.J, Cooke, P. and Heidenreich, M(ed.)

Cooke, P., (1998c). Regional systems of innovation: an evolutionary perspective, *Environment & Planning* A, 30.

Cooke, P. & Morgan, K. (1998) *The Associational Economy*: Firms, Regions, and Innovation, Oxford Univ. Press.

Cortada, James W. (2000) *21st Century Business*: Managing and Working in the New Digital Economy Prentice Hall

Cox, R.W.(1993). "Structural Issues of Global Governance." In S. Gil ed. *Historical Materialism and International Relations*. Cambridge: Cambridge University Press.

Debresson, C. and F. Amesse (1991). "Networks of Innovators: A Review and Introduction to the Issue". *Research Policy*. Special Edition.

Dosi, G. (1988). "Sources, Procedures, and Microeconomic Effects of Innovation". *Journal of Economic Literature*. 26. September.

Drucker, Peter. (1998). "The Discipline of Innovation". *Harvard Business Review*. Nov-dec.

DTI (Department of Trade and Industry, United Kingdom), 2001, *Business Clusters in the UK*: A First Assessment, Cluster Mapping Report.

Emmerij, Louis, "Globalization, Regionalization and World Trade", *Columbia Journal of World Business.* Summer 1992 Vol 27., No.2.

European Commssion (1995). *Managing Science and Technology in the Regions.* Proceedings of the 5th STRIDE conference.

Farazmand, Ali(1999). "Globalization and Public Administration". *Public Administration Review.* 59(6). 509-522.

Ferguson, Thomas and James K. Galbraith, "The American wage Structure 1920-1947", Mimeo. The University of Texas at Austin. 1997.

Fischer, M. (1999). "The innovation process and network activities of manufacturing firms", in Fischer, M et. al. (eds), *Innovation, Networks and Localities*, Springer., pp. 11-27.

Fischer, M. M., J. R. Diez & F. Snickars, (2001).*Metropolitan Innovation systems*, Springer

Fox, J.(1996). "How does Civil Society thinken?,": The Political Construction of Social Capital in Rural Mexico. *World Development.* Vol. 24. Issue 6.

Freeman, C.(1991). "The Nature of Innovation and the Evolution of the Production System", in OECD Report *Technology and Productivity: Challenges for Economic Policy*, Paris.

Freeman, C. (1987). "The Challenge of New Technologies". in *Interdependence and Co-operation in Tomorrow's World.* OECD, Paris.
Farok, Contractor J., "Technology Importation Policies in Developing Countries: Some Implications of Recent Theoretical and Empirical Evidence," Journal of Developing Areas, Vol 117, 1983, pp.449-520.

Freeman, C. (1987). *Output measurement in Science & Technology*, North-Holland, Amsterdam.

Fritsch, M., (2001). Co-operation in Regional Innovation Systems, *Regional Studies*, 35(4), 297-307

Fuentes, Carlos, "Embracing NAFTA and 21st Century", *World Press Review*. Nov.1993. Vol 40., no.11.

Galbraith, James K. and Junmo Kim (1998) "The Legacy of the Heavy and Chemical Industrialization in Korea" Journal of Economic Development Vol. 23(1).

Galbraith, James K. and Junmo Kim (2001) "Legacy of the Korean Industrial Policy," Chapter 13 in Inequality & Industrial Change, Cambridge University Press

Galbraith, James K. and P. Calmon, "Wage Change and Trade Performance in U.S. Manufacturing Industries", *Cambridge Journal of Economics*. Vol 20. No. 4. July: 433-450.

Geoffrey Garret. "The transition to Economic and Monetary Union", in Barry Eichengreen and Jeffrey Frieden eds., (1998), *Forging an Integrated Europe*. The University of Michigan Press.

Gerschenkron, Alexander., Economic Backwardness in Historical Perspective, Cambridge, Massachusetts: Harvard University Press. 1962.

Gershon, Diane (1999). "How to win Venture Capital Financing." *Nature*. May 1999.

Giaccaria, Paolo, (1999) Learning and competitiveness: the case of Turin, *Geo journal*, 49(4), pp 401-410

Gibson, David.(2004) editor. *Learning and Knowledge for the Network Society*, Purdue University Press. (forthcoming April)

Gibson, D. V. & E.M. Rogers (1994). *R&D Collaboration on Trial*. Harvard Business School Press. Boston, Mass.

Goldthorpe, John H. (1968). *The Affluent Worker:* Industrial Attitudes and Behavior. Cambridge University Press, London.

Gong-Bo-Cheau (1997). *2002 International comparative survey of civic attitudes*. Seoul, Korea.

Grayson, L. (1993). *Science Parks: An Experiment in High Technology Transfer*. The British Library, London.

Greenwood, John, "Potential for an Asian Trade Area", *Business Economics*. Jan 1990 Vol 25. No.1.

Gunston, Bill., (ed.), The Encyclopedia of Modern War Planes: The Development and Specifications of All Active Military Aircraft, New York: Barnes & Noble Books. 1995, pp.36-37

Hamel, G., Y. Doz, & C. K. Prahalad (1989). "Collaborate with your Competitors and Win". *Harvard Business Review*. 1.

Harrison, Bennet (1994) Lean & Mean: The Changing Landscape of Corporate Power in the Age of Flexibility. New York Basic Books.

Harriss, John.(1997). "Policy arena: Missing Link or Analytically Missing?: The Concept of Social Capital," *Journal of International Development*. Vol.9. no.7.

Hassink, Robert.(2000). "Regional Innovation Support System in South Korea and Japan", *Zeitschrift fur Wirtschaftsgeographie* Jg. 44.

Heady, Ferrel.(1979). *Public Administration*: A Comparative Perspective. Marcel Dekker.

Hipple, E Von. (1987). "Cooperation between Rivals: Informal Know-how Trading". *Research Policy*. 16(6).

Hong, Gi-Seok (1999) "An Empirical Study on the cause of the financial crisis" (in Korean) KDI Policy studies series.

Hudson, R, (1994). Institutional Change, Culture transformation and Economic regeneration: Myths and Realities from Europe's Old industrial

Areas, in Amin, A & N Thrift (eds), *Globalization, Institution and Regional Development in Europe*, Oxford University Press, Oxford, 196-216

International Institute for Management Development(IMD) (various years) *World Competitiveness Yearbook.*

Joo, Jae Hyun (1999). *An Examination of the Public Service Charter Program in Korea*: Searching for an Effective Operation System. The Korea Institute of Public Administration. Seoul, Korea. (in Korean)

Kahler, Miles, "A World of Blocs: Facts and Factoids", *World Policy Journal.* Spring 1995. Vol 12. No.1.

Katz, Lawrence F., and Lawrence Summers. "Industry Rents: Evidence and Implications." *Brookings Papers on Economic Activity: Microeconomics 1989.* Washington, D.C.: Brookings Institution 1989.

Kawamoto, T. (1992). "An Assessment of Science Cities: Lesson from the Experience of Tsukuba Science City." *Proceedings of the International Symposium on the Development Strategies for Science Town.* Daejon.

KDI Economic Outlook 2001 Seoul, Korea. Korea Development Institute

Keeble, David, Clive Lawson, Barry Moore and Frank Wilkinson, (1999).Collective Learning Process, Networking and Institutional Thickness in the Cambridge Region, *Regional Studies*, 33(4), 319-332

Keohane, Robert and Joseph Nye, Power and Interdependence: World Politics in Transition. Boston Little Brown & Company 1977.

Killing, J. Peter., "Technology Acquisition: License Agreement or Joint Venture," Columbia Journal of World Business, Vol. 15, Fall 1980, pp.38-46.

Kim, Junmo., "An Empirical Approach to Korean Industrial Policy," A Paper presented at the First International conference on Technology Policy and Innovation. Macau. 1997.

Kim, Junmo. (1997) Macro Evaluation of the Korean Industrial Policy: A Wage Analysis based on Discriminant Analysis. Ph.D. Dissertation. LBJ School of Public Affairs, University of Texas at Austin Dec. 1997

Kim, Junmo (1999) "Firm Size and Inequality of Government Policy"(in Korean) The Korea Public Administration Journal. Seoul, Korea: The Korea Institute of Public Administration.

Kim, Junmo (1999) "Firm size and Inequality in Government policy" *The Korea Public Administration Journal.* The Korea Institute of Public Administration. Seoul, Korea. (in Korean)

Kim, Junmo (2000) "Empirical Approach to the Korean Industrial Policy". in Pedro Conceição, David Gibson, Manuel V. Heitor, and Syed Shariq eds. *Science, Technology, and Innovation Policy*: Opportunities and Challenges for the Knowledge Economy

Kim, Junmo (2001) "Economic Integration of Major Industrialized Areas: An Empirical Tracking of the Continued Trend" Technological Forecasting & Social Change Vol 67(2-3) pp.188-202.

Kim, Junmo (2002) *The South Korean Economy* Ashgate Publishing. Aldershot England

Kim, Junmo (2002). "Network Building between research institutions and Small & Medium enterprises(SMEs): dynamics of innovation network building and implications for a policy option", *International Journal of Technology, Policy, Management,* Vol. 2. No.3.

Kim, Junmo (2005) "Are Industries destined toward Productivy Paradox", International Journal of Technology Mangement(IJTM) Vol. 29, no.3/4

Kim, Linsu (1997). *Imitation to Innovation*: The Dynamics of Korea's Technological Learning. Boston: Harvard Business School Press.

Kim, Linsu (2000). "Public Sector Reform in Korea," A paper presented at the *International Conference on Public Sector Reform*: Challenges and Vision for the 21$^{st}$ century. Organized by the Korea Institute of Public Finance(KIPF) and OECD. Seoul, Korea June 22-23, 2000.

Korea Association for Electronics Industry Promotion, *Korea Electronics Industry Yearbook 2002*

Korten, David (1995). *When Corporations rule the World.* West Hartford, CT: Kumarian Press.

Koschatzky, K & M. Kulicke. (1994). "Policies towards Technology based companies in a regional context," in Gonda F. Sakauchi ed. *Regionalization of Science and Technology Resources in the context of Globalization.*

Krugman, Paul. (1996). *Domestic Distortions and Deindustrialization Hypothesis.* Cambridge, Mass.

Lagendijk, A, (1997). 'From new industrial spaces to regional innovation systems and beyond: how and from whom should industrial geography learn?', *EUNIT Discussion Paper* 10, Newcastle upon Tyne: CURDS, University of Newcastle upon Tyne.

Lee, Hyung-Koo (1996) Korean Economy: Perspective for the 21$^{st}$ century Albany, New York State University of New York Press

Levi, Lucio. "Recent Development in Federalist Theory," *The Federalist*, No. 2(1987).

Levy, J. D. & R.J. Samuels. (1991). "Research Collaboration as Technology Strategy." in Mytelka ed. *Strategic Partnerships.* Pinter Publishers, London.

Liebowitz, Stan(2002) *Re-Thinking the Network Economy*: The True Forces That Drive the Digital Marketplace AMACOM

Lipsky, Michael Street Level Bureaucracy

*Lloyd's Shipping Economist.* Lloyd's of London Press Ltd. Each Year from 1988 through 1997.

Lorenz, E & C Lawson, (1999). Collective Learning, Tacit Knowledge and Regional Innovative Capacity, *Regional Studies,* 33(4), 305-318

Luger, M.I. (1994). "Critical Success Factors for High Tech Development Policy: Science Park/Innovation Centers in the U.S.". *Proceedings of NISTEP Conference on Regionalization of Science and Technology Resources in the context of Globalization.*

Luger, M.I.(1994). "Critical Success Factors for High Tech Development Policy Science Park/Innovation Centers in the U.S.", *Proceedings of NISTEP on regionalization of science & technology resources in the context of globalization.*

Lundvall, B & P Maskell, (2000). Nation States and Economic Development: From National systems of Production To National Systems of Knowledge creation and Learning, in Clark, G. L. et al. (eds), *The Oxford Handbook of Economic Geography*, Oxford University Press, Oxford, 353-372

Lundvall, B. A. (1992). *National Systems of Innovation.* Pinter Publishers, London.

Lynch, R. P. (1990). *The Practical Guide to Joint Ventures & Corporate Alliance.*

Markusen, A.R.(1997). "Sticky Places in Slippery Space: a typology of Industrial District", *Economic Geography*

Maskell P & E J Malecki, (2002).The Evolution of technologies in time and Space: From National and Regional to Spatial innovation Systems, *International Regional Science Review*, 25(1), 102-131

Masser, I. (1989). "Technology and Regional Development". *Regional Studies.* 24.

Masser, I. (1991). "By Accident or Design: Some Lessons from Technology Led Local Economic Development Initiatives." *Review of Urban and Regional Development Studies.* 3.

McKay, David.. *Rush to Union: Understanding the European Federal Bargain*, Oxford: Clarendon Press 1996.

Metcalfe, S. (1990). "On Diffusion, Investment, and the Process of Technological Change," in Deiaco et al. *Technology and Investment: Critical Issues for the 1990s*. Pinter Publishers, London.

Minshall, C.W.(1983). "An Overview of Trends in Science & High Technology Parks", *Economic and Policy Analysis Occasional Papers*, No. 37.

Monck, C. S., Porter, R. B., P. Qunitas & D. J. Storey. (1988). *Science Parks and the Growth of High Technology Firms*. Routlege.

Murphy, Alexander B., "Economic Regionalization and Pacific Asia", *The Geographical Review*. April 1995. Vol 85. No.2.

National Business Incubation Association(NBIA) (1998). *State of the Business Incubation Report.*

NBIA (1997). *Business Incubation works: Results from the impact of Incubator Investments Study.*

Nelson, Richard., High Technology Policies: A Five Nation Comparison, Washington and London: American Enterprise Institute for Public Policy Research. 1984.

Nelson, R. (1993). *National Innovation System: A Comparative Analysis.* Oxford University Press.

Nelson, R. & Romer, P. (1996). "Science, Economic Growth and Public Policy", in B.L.R. Smith and C.E. Barfield eds. *Technology, R&D, and the Economy*. Brookings Institution, Washington, D.C.

Nobelius, D. (2004) "Towards the sixth generation of R&D management", International Journal of R&D Management Vol. 22.

Norton, R.D. (1986) "Industrial Policy and American Renewal", Journal of Economic Literature, Vol 24. March.

OECD (1989). *Education in OECD Countries*. Paris.

OECD (1997). *National Innovation System*. Paris.

OECD (1995). *Governance in Transition*: Public Management Reforms in OECD Countries. Paris: OECD.

OECD (1993). *Public Management*: OECD Country Profiles. Paris. Public Management Service (PUMA).
OECD, (1999a). *Managing National Innovation Systems*.

OECD, (1999b). *Boosting Innovation*: The Cluster Approach.

OECD, (2001). *Innovative Clusters*: Drivers of National Innovation Systems.

OECD. *National Innovation System*: Paris OECD 1997.

Office of Government Policy Coordination(OGPM). (1999). Corruption in Korea: The Roots and Extent. A KIPA Contract research funded by OGPM

Oh, D.S. & I. Masser. (1995). "High Tech Centers and Regional Innovation". *Habitat International*. 19(3).

Ohmae, Kenichi (1990). *The Borderless World*. London: Harper-Collins.

O'Loughlin, John, Luc Anselin, "Geo-Economic Competition and Trade Bloc Formation: United States, German, Japanese Exports, 1968-1992. *Economic Geography*, April. 1996. Vol 72. No.2.

Oosterhaven, Jan, Gerard J Eding, Dirk Stelder, (2001). Cluster, Linkage and Interregional Spillover: Methodology and Policy Implication for the Two Dutch Main ports and the Rural North,*Regional Studies* Vol 35. 9, pp 809-822

Osborne, D. and Gaebler, T. (1993). *Reinventing Government: How the Entrepreneurial Spirit is Transforming the Public Sector.* London: Plume.

Pearson, R. (1990). "Scientific Research Manpower: A Review of Supply and Demand Trends". Institute of Manpower. *Studies Report.* 169. University of Sussex. U.K.

Perez, C. and C. Freeman (1988). "Structural Crises of Adjustment, Business Cycles and Investment Behavior", in Dosi, G., C Freeman, R. Nelson, and G. Silverberg and L. Soete eds. *Technical Change and Economic Theory.* Pinter Publishers, London.

Perrin, J. (1988). "Local Synergies and Regional Policies in Europe in High Technology Industry and Innovative Environments: The European Experience". Aydolot et al ed. *Routledge,* London.

Piore, Michael and Charles Sable, The Second Industrial Divide, New York: Basic Books. 1984.

Piore, Michael & Charles Sabel. (1984). *The Second Industrial Divide.* Basic Books. New York.

Piore, Michael and Charles Sabel, (1984). *The Second Industrial Divide,* Basic Books, New York.

Pisano, G.(1989). "Using Equity Participation to support Exchange: Evidence from the Biotechnology Industry", *Journal of Law, Economics, and Organization.*

Porter, Michael. E. (1998). "Clusters and the New Economics of Competititon". *Harvard Business Review.* Nov.-Dec.

Porter M. E, (1998a). 'Clusters and the new economics of competition', *Harvard Business Review,* November-December, vol 76, no 6, pp 77-90

Porter M. E, (1998b). "The Adam Smith Address", *Business Economics,* vol. 33, no.1

Peak, Martha H., "Misconceptions about NAFTA", *Management Review.* March 1993. Vol 82. No.3.

Powell, W.W. (1990). "Neither Market nor Hierarchy: Network Forms of Organization," in B, Straw and Cummings eds. *Research in Organizational Behavior.* 12(3).

Price, C. (1994). "Economic Regulation of Privatized Monopolies," in P.M. Jackson and C.M. Price eds. *Privatization and Regulation*: A Review of the Issues. London: Longman.

Putnam, Robert D. (1993*). Making Democracy Work*: Civic Traditions in Modern Italy Princeton, NJ: Princeton University Press

Putnam, Robert D. (1995). "Bowling Alone: America's Declining Social Capital," *Journal of Democracy* 6:1. Jan.

Rantisi, N. M., (2002). The Local Innovation System as a Source of Variety: Openness and Adaptability in New York City's Garment District, *Regional Studies*, 36(6), 587-602

Reid, Gavin C. (1993a). *Small Business Enterprise: an economic analysis.* London Routledge.

Reid, Gavin C. & Margo E. Anderson (1993b). *Profiles in Small Business.* London Routledge.

Riggs, Fred.(1964). *Administration in Developing Countries*: The Theory of Prismatic Society. Houghton Mifflin Co.

Rosenberg, Nathan. (1982). *Inside the Black Box: Technology and Economics.* Cambridge University Press.

Rosenberg, Nathan. & Nelson, R.(1996). "The Roles of Universities in the Advance of Industrial Technology", in R.S. Rosenbloom and W.J. Spencer eds. *Engines of Innovation*, Harvard Business School Press, Cambridge, MA.

Rothwell, R. (1984). "Technology-based Small Firms and Regional Innovation Potential: The Role of Public Procurement". *Journal of Public Policy.* 4(4). Nov.

Ruhli, Edwin, Stefan Schuppisser, "Switzerland and Its Industry in International Competition", *Columbia Journal of World Business.* Winter 1994. Vol 29. No.4.

Rullani, E. and Zanfei. (1988). "Networks between Manufacturing and Demand: Cases from Textile and Clothing Industries". in Antonelli ed. *New Information Technology and Industrial Change.* Kluwer Academic publishers., Dordrecht.

Sakong, Il editor (1987) *Macroeconomic Policy and Industrial Development Issues* Seoul, KDI

Sandholtz, W. (1992). *High Tech Europe: The Politics of International Cooperation. University of California Press.*, Berkeley, Calif.

Saxenian, A., (1994). *Regional Advantage*: Culture and Competition in Silicon Valley and Route 128, Harvard University Press.

Schrader, S. (1991). "Information Technology Transfer between Firms:Co-operation through Information trading". *Research Policy.* 20(2).

Segal, Quince. (1985). *The Cambridge Phenomenon: The growth of High Tech Industry in a University Town.* Cambridge.

Senyo, John (2002) *Digital Bridges*: Developing Countries in the Knowledge Economy: Idea Group Publishing

Shimada, H. (1991). "Humanware, Technology, and Industrial Relations". in *Technology and Productivity.* OECD, Paris.

Shin, In Seok (1999) "Korea's Financial Crisis: a study on the mechanism" KDI policy studies series. Seoul, Korea. Korea Development Institute.

Shy Oz (2001) *The Economics of Network Industries* Cambridge University Press.

Slottje, D.J., Joseph G. Hirschberg, and Esfandiar Massoumi, "Cluster Analysis for Measuring Welfare and Quality of Life Across Countries". Journal of Econometrics 50 (1991): 131-150.

Statistical Bureau of Korea, *Manufacturing & Extraction Statistics Report*, each year

Sung, T.K. (1997). "Comparative Study of the Development Strategy of Technopolis in Korea". The first International Conference on Technology Policy and Innovation. July, 1997. Macau.

Swan, G.M.P, Prevezer M, Stout D(eds), (1998). *The Dynamics of Industrial Clustering*, Oxford University Press.

Tapscott, Don (1995) *The Digital Economy*: Promise and Peril in the Age of Networked Intelligence McGraw-Hill Trade

Tapscott, Don (1999) *Creating Value in the Network Economy* Harvard Business School Press Cambridge, Mass

Tapscott, Don, David Ticoll, David Ticoll, Alex Lowy (2000) Harnessing the Power of Business Webs Harvard Business School Press. Cambridge, Mass.

Tatsuno, S. (1986). *The Techno Polis Strategy:Japan, High Technology and the control of the 21st century*. Prentice Hall. New York.

Timothy Bresnahan, Alfonso Gambardella, Annalee Saxenian, (2001). Old Economy Inputs for New Economy Outcomes: Clusters Formation in the New Silicon Valleys, *Industrial and Corporate Change*, 10(4), pp 835-860

Waltz, Kenneth. *Theory of International Politics*, Reading: Addison-Wesley. 1979.

Ward, J.H. "Hierarchical Grouping to optimize objective function." *Journal of the American Statistical Association* 58. 1963

Weizsacker, Carl Christian Von., Barriers to Entry: A Theoretical Treatment, New York: Springer-Verlag. 1980.

Welch, Eric & Wilson Wong(1998). "Public Administration in a Global Context: Bridging the Gaps of Theory and Practice between Western and Non-Western Nations". *Public Administration Review.* 58(1). 40-49.

Wijangco, Mayen., "B.J Habibies: Achieving a Technology Take-Off," World Executive's Digest, April 1989, pp.22-25.

World Economic Forum. (2004, 2000,1997). *Global Competitiveness Report.*

Yamawaki Hideki (2002). The Evolution and Structure of Industrial Clusters in Japan, *Small Business Economics* 18, no 1/3, pp 121-140.

Yip, George., Barriers to Entry: A Corporate Strategy Perspective, Lexington, Massachusetts: Lexington Books. 1982.

Yoo, C. W. and Junmo Kim (2005) "Recovering from Science: How far can we push?" International Journal of Technology Management (IJTM) Vol .29., no. 3/4/Jan.

# Index

**A**

Asian countries 3, 17, 20, 25, 38, 39, 40, 42, 45, 46, 47, 49, 50, 52, 87, 104, 121

Auto Industry 27, 28, 29, 30, 31, 42, 51

**B**

Best Practice 123, 132, 135

**C**

Cluster 11, 14, 19, 20, 21, 23, 24, 25, 28, 29, 32, 33, 36, 37, 40, 41, 45, 46, 49, 60, 61, 62, 66, 67, 73, 74, 82, 83, 105, 106, 107, 108, 136, 137, 139, 143, 145, 154, 158

Computer 4, 75, 101, 103, 107, 108, 111

**D**

Digital Economy 98, 99, 101, 105, 106, 144, 145, 158

**E**

Economic Blocs 2, 14, 15, 16, 19, 20, 23, 24, 29, 51, 52, 53, 136, 137

Economic Determinism 1, 2, 3, 16, 17

Electronics 14, 18, 45, 46, 47, 48, 51, 52, 53, 58, 89, 90, 102, 103, 104, 105, 114, 151

**F**

Fabricated Metal 18, 32, 33, 34, 35, 36, 37, 52, 53, 108

Flexible Specialization 8, 60, 64, 65, 86

France 7, 8, 12, 20, 36, 40, 45, 59, 73, 75, 76, 77, 102, 103, 130, 133

**G**

Globalization xv, 1, 2, 3, 14, 16, 17, 29, 51, 87, 115, 116, 118, 124, 125, 126, 128, 129, 136, 137, 143, 144, 146, 149, 151, 152

Government policy 97, 127, 150, 154

**I**

Incentives 3, 4, 9, 10, 67, 99, 100, 111, 117, 118, 123, 129

Industrial Development xv, 1, 19, 157

Industrial machinery 18, 37, 39

Industrial Policy 3, 4, 29, 87, 88, 99, 100, 103, 116, 147, 149, 150, 153

Infra structure 4, 77, 78, 98, 99, 100, 101, 102, 106, 107, 108, 111, 112, 113, 114

Innovation 11, 12, 13, 60, 61, 63, 65, 66, 67, 68, 69, 73, 74, 77, 80, 82, 83, 87, 89, 97, 116, 143, 145, 146, 148, 149, 150, 151, 152, 153, 154, 156, 157, 158

**K**

Kista 73, 74, 75

Knowledge Economy 5, 11, 150, 157

Korean government 4, 101, 112, 124, 126, 128, 130

## M
Man power 70, 71, 79

## N
NAFTA 20, 21, 24, 25, 26, 27, 29, 31, 32, 33, 38, 40, 42, 49, 50, 52, 136, 147, 156
National issues 70, 71
Network 11, 13, 61, 62, 63, 66, 67, 68, 69, 75, 78, 80, 81, 82, 83, 84, 86, 87, 88, 89, 90, 91, 92, 93, 94, 95, 96, 97, 111, 146, 147, 150, 151, 156, 158
New Zealand 21, 130, 132, 133, 134, 135
NPM 129, 130, 135

## O
Olson Mancur 9, 117

## P
PC 103, 104, 105, 111
Policy Implication 59, 71, 81, 96, 154
Political Determinism 2, 17
Porter Michael 11, 60, 66, 67, 118, 155
Primary Metal 18, 49, 50, 53, 58
Productivity Paradox 5, 6, 61, 69, 71, 72, 80, 85, 86, 87
Public Sector 13, 14, 115, 116, 118, 121, 122, 123, 124, 126, 127, 128, 129, 130, 131, 132, 133, 134, 135, 150, 155

## R
R xv, xvi, 5, 6, 61, 62, 68, 69, 70, 71, 72, 79, 83, 84, 85, 86, 137, 147, 153
R Model 83, 84, 86
Rational choice 9, 123
Recovery 105, 113, 114, 130, 131, 132

Regional Innovation system 12, 13, 60, 61, 65, 68, 69, 145, 146, 151
Regulation xvi, 3, 4, 8, 65, 99, 100, 101, 130, 136, 144, 145, 156

## S
Science Park 11, 12, 60, 61, 62, 63, 69, 87, 148, 152, 153
Shipbuilding 18, 39, 40, 41, 42, 43, 44, 52, 53
SMEs 78, 79, 81, 88, 89, 90, 91, 92, 93, 94, 95, 96, 97, 150
Social Capital 13, 14, 115, 116, 117, 118, 119, 121, 122, 123, 124, 128, 135, 137, 146, 148, 156
Sophia Antipolis 12, 63, 64, 75, 76, 77, 78, 79
Sweden 32, 36, 40, 45, 54, 59, 73, 74, 75, 133

## T
Technopole 62, 63
Technopolis 11, 12, 60, 62, 63, 65, 68, 158
Textile 18, 24, 25, 26, 27, 37, 42, 52, 53, 55, 108, 157
Trust 12, 13, 62, 64, 65, 88, 90, 92, 93, 94, 95, 96, 97, 100, 118

## U
U.S. Money Supply 14, 23, 24, 25, 26, 29, 31, 33, 38, 39, 41, 42, 43, 44, 46, 47, 48, 49, 50, 51, 137

## W
Wage 3, 14, 15, 18, 19, 20, 23, 25, 26, 29, 33, 38, 40, 43, 46, 47, 50, 51, 52, 53, 105, 106, 136, 139, 140, 146, 147, 150

978-0-595-36098-7
0-595-36098-X

www.ingramcontent.com/pod-product-compliance
Lightning Source LLC
Chambersburg PA
CBHW020418290526
45785CB00002B/613